I0162201

The Arlesey Fossil Diggings

Bernard O'Connor

Few people are aware that fossil digging was once a lucrative occupation in Arlesey. In the late-1850s a new industry started in the fields nearby which provided an alternative occupation to agricultural work. It was digging up coprolite, locally called "fossiling." What follows is an examination of the social, economic and religious impact that this unusual industry had on Arlesey and surrounding parishes.

Until the nineteenth century Arlesey and the surrounding parishes in the Clifton Hundred were small agricultural communities that had not changed much since the Middle Ages. Things were about to change. Something happened in the second half of the century that very much brought it into the Victorian era of industrial and economic change. Whilst most of the villagers were engaged as agricultural labourers on the local farms others were employed in associated trades with millers, carters, wheelwrights, brewers and carpenters. Shopkeepers and beersellers thrived and many women and girls got employment in plaiting and domestic service. The gentry, like the Edwards family of Etonbury Manor and Henlow Grange, lived in style with butlers, maids and a governess whilst most villagers lived in small, cramped, thatched cottages with a small garden for growing fruit and vegetables, keeping a pig and chickens.

Few people had well-paid employment and for many life was simply trying to make ends meet year after year. C. E. Hanscomb's history of Shillington parish describes this period as one of a difficult, harsh existence for many.

> *"Rents and tithes had risen with the price of corn... the harsh game laws, involving transportation for offenders, were of the utmost danger to the working classes and, coupled with the corn laws, showed the influence of the landowners on the government. It was illegal to kill game. Spring guns and mantraps were legal until 1827. Until the repeal of the Corn Laws in 1846 farmers and their workers suffered from the constantly fluctuating prices. Food was dear, bread, cheese, and potatoes,*

with an occasional bit of fat pork, were the farm labourers' chief foods. Serious labour troubles were frequent in town and country alike."

(Hanscomb, C. E. (1967), *'Common Blood,'* Queen Anne Press, pp.158-9)

Life in agricultural communities was not the quiet and peaceful rural idyll that characterised traditional images of country life. There were tremendous economic and social changes brought about in the nineteenth century. The introduction of the Enclosures after 1799 and the implementation of the new technology introduced during the "Agricultural Revolution" had a dramatic impact on rural villages. Many farm labourers became entirely dependent of the farmers for their livelihood. There were "hiring fairs" where men and women were taken on according to the decoration of their lapel. The historian, David Ellison, referred to this period and commented on the "startling" social effects which resulted.

"The repeal of the Corn Laws and the lower prices of corn for farmers had made them all try to save costs by mechanisation and reducing their labour forces. Little wonder that the first section of the Mormon church in this part of England, outside Bedford, had its first headquarters there - they encouraged and advanced money, for men to emigrate with their families across the Atlantic to a promised land - and, oddly enough, one of the appeals of their church was that almost anyone could become a priest in it. Cambridge's farm labourers had often noticed the immense gulf between themselves with their £25 to £30 a year, and the rectors with £300 - £400, comfortable rectories, and often land as well as house servants."

(Ellison, D. 'Coprolites in the Orwell area,' part of *Orwell History Topics*; Ref. Latter Day Saints Millennial Star, passim, and Kowallis, Gay P. (1970?), *'To the Great Salt Lake from Litlington,'* Bassingbourn)

As farm labourers they tended to live in tied cottages which they could easily be evicted from at the whim of the farmer or farm bailiff. Not being seen at church for the Sunday service was a dismissible offence. Afterwards they had to wait by the door of the pub until the Lord of the Manor went in. There was considerable poverty and overcrowding in crumbling "shit and stubble" or wattle and daub thatched cottages in many rural villages. New steam-powered agricultural machinery, designed to save time and labour, was introduced by farmers who were keen to profit from the increased demand for food. These machines like the steam traction engine, threshing machine, deep plough and elevator resulted in an increasing number of redundancies in farm labour. Some developed useful mechanical skills but there was widespread unrest in most rural communities. Many landless peasants were forced off the land when they lost the right to use the open fields. The loss of gleaning rights after harvest, the loss of the common for grazing animals and poultry, the denial of access to the newly fenced or walled in woodland reduced their "free" catch of rabbit, pheasant, partridge, nuts and wild fruit.

The unrest was manifested in Stotfold where on Wednesday December 2nd 1830. A group of labourers marched to the houses of the local gentry and demanded an increase in wages to two shillings (£0.05) a day, to be exempt from the parish rates and for the overseer to be sacked. A meeting was arranged at the vestry the following day and all the men and boys at the local farms were called to join the demonstration. Up to two hundred assembled and although some of their requests were allowed the farmers refused to increase their wages. This sparked a riot in which the infuriated assembly demanded bread from the bakers, beer from the publicans and money from the inhabitants. Buildings were broken into and items taken. In the evening they set fire to stubble in a field and told the farmers that if their demands were not met by the Saturday there would be further violence.

The local gentry reacted with force. William Whitbread and Rev. John Hull the local magistrates swore in a considerable number of special constables from neighbouring villages. The Lord-Lieutenant of Bedford sent more than a hundred others and in less than half an hour ten of the ring leaders were arrested and taken to Bedford gaol. In March the following year they were all found guilty and sentences ranged from six weeks to a year's imprisonment. Three were sentenced to death but these were commuted to transportation for life. (Phillips, Rev. G. C. H. (1951), 'Stotfold, Beds.' Bancroft Press, Hitchin, pp.34-36)

Over the first half of the century many parishes in this area experienced dramatic population increases. The completion of the Great Northern and the Bedford and Hitchin branch of the Midland Railways in the 1850s stimulated small-scale industrial development with coal and gas businesses being established in the goods yards at Shefford Station for example. Messrs. S. Owens and Company established an engineering works in Arlesey. It is said that many Irish "navvies", labourers who were involved in building the railway, gained employment locally. Entrepreneurs invested capital to exploit the local gault clay to make bricks for the housing developments taking place in the settlements near the railways. Arlesey, only four miles north of Hitchin, grew up alongside what is claimed to be the longest High Street in the country. Its population increased almost 250% from 1801 to 1401 in 1861. Over the same period Stotfold's population increased 318% to 2071 and Clifton's increased 350% to 1478. All the other local settlements saw similar significant increases. The only one to experience a decline was Astwick whose numbers fell from 99 in 1821 to 64 in 1861. (BCRO. Census returns)

Better-paid factory or domestic work enticed the more motivated sections of the community, mainly young adult males and females, to find employment in the industrial towns and cities. Most of those who were unable to leave were employed on the farms where new technology meant many lay offs. Some manifested their dissatisfaction with the state of affairs by acts of vandalism. This period, known as "The Swing", after the number of hangings of offenders, saw incidences of farm machinery being destroyed and haystacks, barns and even farmers' houses being set alight. (Fowle, K. (19--), *Coton through the Ages*') However, the discovery of a fossil seam running across the area reduced this unrest.

As shall be seen, this dissatisfaction diminished during the coprolite years with higher wages and a variety of new jobs available. What were these coprolites? "Coprolites," as they were called when they were first discovered, were thought to be fossilised droppings. There are numerous variations of their spelling, due in part to the poor literacy of the census enumerator but also to variations in local dialect. They include coprolite, copperlight, copper light, copperlite, coupperlite, copralite, corporolite, coprelite, coperlite, coporlite, coproilite, coparlite, coprolithe and coperalite. No wonder there was confusion over their origin. (Analysis of the 1861 – 1891 census data) The word came from the Greek "kopros" meaning dung and "lithos" meaning stone. Dung stone - fossilised droppings! It was first coined by Rev. William Buckland, the Dean of Westminster when he was the first professor of Geology and Mineralogy at the University of Oxford. In 1829 he went on a geological excursion to the Dorset coast at Lyme Regis. Examining the clay and sands exposed by a recent landslip he found the complete fossil remains of an ichthyosaurus. Unusually, it also included its fossilised stomach contents.

Accompanying him on the excursion was the German analytical chemist, Baron Von Justus Liebig. He too was fascinated with the finds but the Dean was obsessed. He had a tabletop inlaid with polished coprolites as well as earrings made from polished slices! It is unknown if he wore them! His dinner parties were very entertaining. A bear used to wander around the dining room behind his guests and a monkey sat on furniture near the window. The menu often included samples from across the food chain, starting from plants and working through the animal kingdom! The worst tasting were reportedly moles and bluebottles! Dinnertime conversations included a challenge to the established religious circles. Buckland had found tiny bones of baby ichthyosaurus in the coprolites. This meant that ichthyosaurus ate ichthyosaurus. They were cannibals! This contradicted the fundamental religious belief that life before Adam was one of peace and harmony. Presumably it was believed that Adam and Eve frolicked with dinosaurs in Eden. Maybe the issue was discussed over dinner with Mr and Mrs Mantell who were the first to find Iguanodon remains in Sussex in 1822 and Sir Richard Owen who first came up with the word dinosaur to mean "terrible lizard". Owen was just as eccentric. On New Year's Eve 1853 he invited twenty scientists to a dinner party inside a life-size model of an iguanodon in a London park!

A similar discovery but one with far reaching implications was made in 1842. After Rev. John Henslow, the professor of Botany at St. John's College, Cambridge had been given a living by St. John's in the Suffolk parish of Hitcham, he went on a trip to the Victorian watering hole of Felixstowe. There had recently been a landslip in which he found some interesting fossils in the newly exposed material at the bottom of the cliffs. There were loads of them. From their smooth, brown, elongated shape he took them to be fossilised dung, similar to those of the ichthyosaurus, discovered by Buckland. (O'Connor, B. (2001), 'The Suffolk Fossil Diggings', Bernard O'Connor, Gamlingay) Aware that a range of animal products were being used as manure he wondered what possible use these fossils could have.

Liebig had done some tests on Buckland's coprolites by dissolving them in vitriol, the then term for sulphuric acid. His analysis of the resultant mass showed them to have a high phosphate content, a mineral much needed in plant growth. John Bennet Lawes, a Hertfordshire landowner, was experimenting with different manures on his estate in Rothamsted. Like Liebig, he too successfully dissolved animal bones, the mineral phosphorite and Felixstowe coprolites in vitriol. The resulting mixture, once dried and bagged, he called "super phosphate of lime". His tests showed that it was soluble in water and that it could rapidly be absorbed by the plant roots. He experiments with it on plants in pots and test beds showed it to be an extremely valuable manure, especially for root crops. His "super" was the world's first artificial chemical manure and its application so dramatically increased turnip yields that it became much in demand by the nation's farmers. They were eager to improve supplies of winter fodder. This was because once the harvest was in and farmers knew how much feedstuffs were available over winter, large numbers of surplus cattle, sheep or pigs had to be slaughtered. Meat commanded higher prices over winter until the new stock was brought onto the market in spring. Any way of providing increased fodder therefore would be very popular with farmers. Those landowners with an icehouse were able to keep their meat longer than the ordinary shopkeeper.

Much to Lawes' pleasure the results of his tests with his new manure showed that it was effective on a whole range of other crops. He patented his "discovery" in 1842, which annoyed Liebig who claimed to have been the first to have done it. It also upset Lawes' mother who was appalled that a gentleman should engage in trade - let alone in manure. Ignoring both he set up his own company. It was called "Lawes Artificial Manure Company." His fiancée could not have been pleased. The planned European Tour for their honeymoon was cancelled in favour of a trip down the Thames during which he spotted an ideal site for his factory. He bought a plot at Deptford and had a large chemical manure works built that was capable of producing up to 200 tons of superphosphate a week. He sold his "super" at up to £7.00 and took legal action against Liebig and others to ensure that anyone who wanted to use his patent had to pay him five shillings (£0.25) for every ton they produced. (Dyke, G.V. (1993), *'John Lawes of Rothamsted'*, Hoos Press, Harpenden, p.15)

Maybe Henslow was in correspondence with Lawes as he realised that the Felixstowe fossil bed could be a valuable source of manure. As a wide range of animal manure was being put onto the fields he thought that fossilised droppings could be used for the same purpose. In 1845 he read a paper in

Cambridge to the British Association for the Advancement of Science. (Henslow, Rev. John, (1845), *Report to British Association*, Cambridge) It dealt with their potential value to the nation's farmers. Suffolk manure manufacturers like William Colchester, Edward Packard and Joseph Fison took interest. They made arrangements with Felixstowe landowners to have the fossils dug up, washed and transported to their works in Ipswich. A few shillings a ton royalty was offered for the fossils. As a cheap alternative to the other manures on the market, there was keen interest in coprolites.

The 18th and 19th century movement from the countryside to the urban industrial areas resulted in an enormous demand for accommodation and food. The ending of the Napoleonic Wars with the defeat of the French at Waterloo in 1815 brought a period of peace and prosperity to Great Britain. Its population doubled over the first half of the century. Towns and cities expanded rapidly on the coalfields and alongside the major rivers and canal system. People were attracted by the employment opportunities in industry, retail and commerce following the inventions of the Industrial Revolution. There were also many forced off the land by the labour saving steam driven machinery introduced during the Agricultural Revolution. The urban population needed feeding. The typical two-up two-down terraced houses didn't have the gardens to grow fruit or vegetables or space to keep a pig or chickens. People needed to buy food from the High Street, the market or the corner shops. Victorian entrepreneurs were quick to recognise the growing demand. Small family businesses dominated the business. As their profits grew they opened more shops, invested in better transport and had more money to buy from the farmers. If farmers could increase production there was more money to be made. Experiments began in an attempt to increase food production.

One can probably remember from one's schooldays Jethro Tull's seed drill, Lord 'Turnip' Townsend's four-course crop rotation method and the Earl of Norfolk and other agriculturalists' crossbreeding produced enormous pigs, cattle and sheep. But other experiments were going on with plants. The application of science and capital was being expended on agriculture as it had been on manufacturing. Once the chemists acknowledged that phosphate was a major nutrient in plant growth, the search was on to discover new supplies. In 1828 a rock phosphate, called phosphorite, started being exploited in Ontario, Canada. Chemists had found its value as a fertiliser and samples were tested in Great Britain. The German explorer, Humboldt, returned to Europe with details of the South American coastline and his report led to the European's "discovering" the use of "huano" or guano. This was an accumulation of tens of feet of phosphate-rich bird droppings that had impregnated discarded fish carcasses and bird skeletons on the Chincha Islands off the coast of Peru. The locals would not excavate it because of the smell so indentured Chinese labour was brought in. Shipping companies started to import it into Liverpool docks from 1838 where it was sold it at up to £12 per ton. This was much more expensive than bones but a successful advertising campaign in the agricultural press led to its widespread usage.

Other experiments included adding a whole range of materials to the soil. Blood, bones, soot, fish, seaweed, chalk, clay and even rags from discarded wool and cotton clothes were trailed. Maybe one can remember the rag and bone man? It was the waste product of the knife manufacturers in Sheffield, however, that sparked the interest in bones. It was found that the shavings from their knife handles proved a very effective fertiliser when added to the soil. (Voelcker, A. (1862), 'The International Exhibition at Paris,' p.149) The corn mills used by the agricultural suppliers were not able to meet the demand for bone meal and this led to the setting up of bone manure works. Their most popular products were half-inch bones. These were burnt or crushed and added to the soil as bone meal.

However, the bones from the knacker's yards were insufficient to meet the demand of the nation's manure manufacturers, a factor that led to the import of dried bones. There were reports of cargoes of mummified cats from Egyptian pyramids and sun-bleached bones from the North African desert and the Argentinean Pampas finding their way into the crushing mills. This was enough to prompt the comment by Baron Von Justus Liebig, that,

>"Great Britain is like a ghoul, searching the continents for bones to feed its agriculture ... robbing all other countries of the condition of her fertility. Already in her eagerness for bones she has turned up the battlefields of Leipzig, Waterloo, and of the Crimea; already from the catacombs of Sicily she has carried away the skeletons of many successive generations."

>(Quoted in Keatley, W.S. (1976), '100 years of Fertiliser Manufacture,' Fertiliser Manufacturers Association; also in Pierre, W.H. and Norman, A.G. (Eds.) (1953), 'Soil Fertiliser Phosphorous in Crop Nutrition', New York Academic Press, p. ix)

By 1839 the bone business was worth £150,000 per annum and about 30,000 tons were being imported annually. The Gardeners' Chronicle and Agricultural Gazette gave detailed accounts of the efficacy of these new manures. (Graham, J. (1839), 'A Treatise on the Use and Value of Manure', London p.6) However, tests showed that crushed bones were insoluble. It also took a long time before their mineral potential could be absorbed. Bones were also expensive and the machinery for grinding them had not been perfected. (Ibid.)

Maybe it was the reports of Rev. Henslow's speech that prompted a local farmer to show him some fossils that he had dug up on his property. Charles Kingsley, one of Henslow's students, must have been present as he recorded Henslow's response.

>"He saw, being somewhat of, a geologist and chemist, that they were not, as fossils usually are, carbonate of lime, but phosphate of lime - bone earth. He said at once, as by

12

inspiration, "You have found a treasure - not a gold-mine, indeed, but a food-mine. This bone earth, which we are at our wit's end to get for our grain and pulses; which we are importing, as expensive bones, all the way from Buenos Ayres. Only find enough of them, and you will increase immensely the food supply of England and perhaps make her independent of foreign phosphates in case of war."

(Anonymous note in Ipswich Museum's Coprolite file)

A treasure? A food-mine? Such a response must have astounded the farmer. It is undocumented where the farmer was from but it is thought that he was from Burwell, a fenland parish north of Cambridge. Fossils had been found beneath the fenland peat from as early as 1816. (Hailstone, Rev. J. (1816), 'Outlines of the Geology of Cambridgeshire', *Phil. Trans. Royal. Soc.*, pp.243-250) Their discovery was related to an important fenland occupation, locally called "claying". This involved the digging of small pits through the "moor" or "bear's muck", as the bog-earth was called, to reach the clay. This lay between two and ten feet (0.74m. - 3.7m.) below the surface. Wearing waterproofed boots the diggers would use a sharp, cutting-edged shovel to dig through the peat, a light wooden scoop to get rid of drainage water and an axe or "bill" to excavate the clay beneath. The top metre of clay was thrown to the sides of the pit and then mixed into the peat.

The material turned up by this "claying" occasionally included fossils of what were thought to be bears and oxen. When Burwell Fen started to be drained in the early-1800s the excavation of drainage ditches or "lodes" exposed an extensive bed of fossils. John Ball, a local farmer, noticed that the turnips he grew on the clayey, fossil deposit that had been mixed into his peat soil produced dramatically better yields than the crops on fields he had not clayed. The Burwell doctor, Mr. Lucas, explained that the "extraordinary liveliness" was related to the high phosphate content of the fossils. ('The Farming of Cambridgeshire', *Royal Agric.Soc.*1847, p.71; Lucas, C. (1930), *'The Fenman's World - Memories of a Fenland Physician'*, (Norwich), p.25)

Dr. Lucas may well have heard about Rev. Henslow's Cambridge speech or read about it in the local press. Aware of the potential demand by manure manufacturers and maybe even knowing the farmer who had shown Henslow the fossils, he suspected that the Burwell deposit could also be a matter of "commercial proposition". Their shallow depth beneath the fenland peat just above the gault clay would allow them to be raised without very high labour costs. The proximity of Burwell Lode allowed easy access by barge or lighter to Popes Corner - the confluence of the Ouse and the Cam - and then via Ely, Littleport and Downham Market onto King's Lynn and then transhipped to Ipswich or London.

With an eye for speculation and without having first seen it, he bought some eleven acres of Burwell Fen. The locals thought he had taken leave of his senses. A month later, so the story goes, he went by boat up Burwell Lode with "an interested party" to locate the deposit. After rowing for some time, they reached a point about a mile west of the village where the potential buyer was handed a "sprit" and told to push it into the land below the boat. (Gathercole, A. F. (1959), 'Fenland Village,' *Fisons Journal*, No.64, Sept. pp.24-9; Suffolk County Record Office (SCRO) HC 438.8728/269)

The depth of the seam was not noted but the locals were astounded when he sold the plot and the coprolites beneath it for £1,000. Realising almost £100 per acre was a phenomenal profit, given that agricultural rents at this time ranged from about ten to forty shillings (£0.50 - £2.00) an acre. The "interested party" was William Colchester, one of the Suffolk manure manufacturers who also had investments in brick manufacturing and ships. In 1846 he expanded his manure business by building a new manure works in Ipswich. According to a later geological paper he had raised 500 tons by 1847. (Lucas, C. (1930), op.cit; Reid, C. (1890), 'Phosphate Nodule Bed', *Memoirs of the Geological Survey (Mem.Geol.Surv.)* p.16)

Others speculated in the new chemical manure industry. Edward Packard, a chemist from Saxmundham in Suffolk successfully processed the Felixstowe "coprolites" and in 1847 he opened his own manure factory on the banks of the River Orwell in Ipswich. Joseph Fison, part of a milling and baking family, had moved into Ipswich in 1840. He established a factory at Stoke Bridge and converted it to process coprolites and other phosphatic material in 1850. (*Fisons Journal*, No.77,December 1963; Norsk Hydro file, Museum of East Anglian Life, Stowmarket)

Lawes, Colchester, Packard and Fison advertised their superphosphate in the pages of the *"Gardeners Chronicle and Agricultural Gazette"* thus realising Henslow's idea. Articles on its successful application and of using coprolites in its manufacture appeared in the agricultural press. These increased landowners and agriculturalists' awareness of the financial advantages of locating the fossil deposit on their properties.

So, by the 1850s, Buckland realised that his discovery had led to the birth of a new industry exploiting fossil beds in Suffolk and Cambridgeshire. He questioned the possibility that these

"...excretions of extinct animals contained the mineral ingredients of so much value in animal manure. The question was in fact not yet solved by the chemist, and we took specimens, in order to confirm by chemical analysis the views of the geologist. After Liebig had completed their analysis, he saw that they might be made applicable to practical purposes.

What a curious and interesting subject for contemplation! In the remains of an extinct animal world England is to find the means of increasing her wealth in *agricultural produce, as she has already found the great support of her manufacturing industry in fossil fuel - the preserved matter of primeval forests - the remains of a vegetable world! May this expectation be realised! and may her excellent population be thus redeemed from poverty and misery!*

I well recollect the storm of ridicule raised by these expressions of the German philosopher, and yet truth has triumphed over scepticism, and thousands of tons of similar animal remains are now used in promoting the fertility of our fields. The geological observer, in his search after evidences of ancient life, aided by the chemist, excavated extinct remains which produced new life to future generations."

(Anonymous author, 'The Study of Abstract Science Essential to the Progress of Industry', *Mem. Geol. Surv.*, Mineral Statistics, Vol. I, 1850?, pp.40-1)

Many people thought that the fossils were the droppings of bear, lizard or fish or even dinosaur droppings. A retired major from Reach thought that they resembled sun-dried wildebeest droppings. They were similar to those he had seen on the banks of the Zambezi once the vast herds had passed. Students and professors at Cambridge University's newly established Geology department became very interested in the range of fossils being thrown up. There was extensive debate in geological circles and many argued that the deposit ought not to be termed coprolite. They should more correctly be termed pseudo-coprolites or phosphatic nodules. However, the trade name "coprolites" stuck. Recently however, an excellent example of some poor creature's rectal content has been found in Barrington that gives credence to the locals' views. One can make out the pressure creases and a sharp point as if it was its last squeeze. Photographs of this and typical Cambridgeshire and Bedfordshire coprolites can be seen in the illustrations.

The bulk of the deposit was of misshapen, black/grey lumps but amongst them were found the teeth, bones, scales and claws of prehistoric creatures such as Cretaceous dinosaurs. They included craterosaurus, dakosaurus, dinotosaurus, megalosaurus, iguanodon and the pterodactyl. Prehistoric marine reptiles of ichthyosaurus, plesiosaurus and pliosaurus were found as well as the remains of whale, shark, turtle and a huge variety of shells, sponges and other marine organisms. The most common was the ammonite. Other animals that were discovered in the diggings included crocodile, hippopotamus, elephant, rhinoceros, lion, hyena, tapir, bear, horse and oxen. (O'Connor, B. (1998), 'The Dinosaurs on Sandy Heath', Bernard O'Connor, Gamlingay) There were also lumps of what some argue are inorganic calcium phosphate. But why is it that such a variety of creatures that you would normally expect to see in hot tropical countries in Africa were found in Bedfordshire?

When the European plate broke away from Pangaea about 500 million years ago it was south of the Equator. It was during this period that the gault clay was deposited. This area was about 28° S, where Namibia is today! To reach its present latitude about 55° N it experienced a range of differing environments on its slow movement north from the tropical and equatorial forests, swamps, savannah grassland and desert to the temperate latitudes. But what had produced such an enormous prehistoric graveyard? A number of the Victorian geologists considered that the Jurassic and Cretaceous fossil deposits had been washed out of the clays which were exposed when the south of England was uplifted from the sea to produce the Weald. A recent theory is that about 94 million years ago sea levels rose dramatically, flooding the London-Brabant Basin, of which present day Bedfordshire formed its north-western coast. It was then situated north of the equator, on the same latitude as the Sahara desert. This inundation wiped out much of the animal population. Carbon dioxide given off by the flood basalts released by the tectonic activity also played their part. Many of the land creatures would have been poisoned and also the marine life that had to come up to the surface for air. Some suggested that as the bodies were washed around as debris in coastal embayments their bones, teeth, scales and claws gradually absorbed the phosphoric acid from overlying deposits of decaying organisms. Another theory was that the calcium absorbed dissolved phosphate from the seawater. It was said that the rivers had dissolved the apatite, a phosphatic mineral found in the volcanic rocks of Scandinavia and Scotland, which impregnated the deposit and explains their higher phosphate content than today's animal and human bones.

Analysis of amber samples shows that at the time when dinosaurs were at their greatest size, about 230 million years ago, the oxygen content of the air was 35%. Over the Cretaceous period it gradually declined as a result of the increased carbon dioxide released into the atmosphere by extensive volcanic activity. Levels fell to 11% 65 million years ago and today they are 21%. Dinosaurs had to adapt to these changing conditions. It was like having asthma, not getting enough oxygen into the blood. They had to build enough energy to catch prey - the "dash and dine" characteristic of today's crocodiles. Many were exhausted, maybe too tired for sex even. Like crocodiles they buried their eggs. It is thought that increased temperatures meant that they had single-sex populations that further reduced numbers. The leathery skin of their eggs absorbed the poisonous gases and embryos failed to develop. In order to survive these changing conditions dinosaurs had to evolve with a much-reduced size. A cataclysmic catastrophe like a rise in sea level of hundreds of feet as well as poisoned air could explain the huge numbers of creatures found in the East Anglian fossil beds. Given the volume of the creatures they must have piled up on each other into a layer many tens of feet thick in hollows on the seabed. The upper bodies would have been eaten by any of the surviving marine life like ammonites and worms but the lower bodies, without oxygen for decomposition, gradually fossilised as the upper layers were covered in the hundreds of feet of Greensand. This was probably washed into the ocean from the arid parts of continent still above sea level.

Compressed by this strata and the subsequent chalk marl they gradually fossilised. This could explain why there are real coprolites in the deposit. The contents of stomachs, intestines and rectums would have been found along with bones, teeth, claws, scales and shells. Throughout the deposit were large numbers of ammonites, squid-like creatures that scavenged on the sea floor but there were oyster shells on the upper surface. Over the millions of years, fluctuations in sea level exposed the soft Greensand and differential erosion uncovered the fossils at its base. The remains would have been washed around, so that one does not find whole skeletons in the deposit. Many of the surface features of the remains were removed by abrasion but lines showing worm tracks are often visible along the nodules, the biggest of which rarely extend over six inches (15cms).

Further inundation resulted in a second bed accumulating which was covered once more with Greensand deposits and then hundreds of feet of chalk. This latter deposit was made up from minute marine organisms whose bodies contained calcium carbonate. When sea levels eventually fell these more recent deposits were exposed the to the elements. The upper layers would have been eroded and the chalk and sand gradually lowered to expose the fossil beds. The sixteen ice ages contributed most to the erosion removing hundreds of feet of rock to leave the low chalk and sandy ridges of East Anglia.

Whilst the bed was one of great fascination to the country's geologists, its commercial value was not in how much they could be sold to those Victorians fascinated by fossils. Another of Rev. Henslow's students at Cambridge was Charles Darwin. His evolutionary theories caused a storm when they were published in 1858 and further stimulated the enormous interest in geology, palaeontology, anthropology and archaeology. Many Victorian drawing rooms had specimens from the Greensand displayed in glass-sided cabinets. They were also eagerly bought up by geology students and their professors as well as by museum curators across the country. Perhaps the best specimens can be found in the Sedgwick Earth Sciences Museum in Cambridge.

Their main value, however, was as a raw material for manure manufacturers. And not just in this country but also overseas. In the late-1840s they were paying landowners as little as a few shillings a ton for them. As more and more businesses joined in the rush for manures demand for coprolite rose. Royalties they paid landowners rose to between seven and fifteen shillings a ton in the early 1850s. They depended on a range of factors. The depth, extent, continuity of the seam, the angle of dip, its cleanliness, the nearness to a water source, road, wharf or station, the volume coming onto the market, knowledge or ignorance of current prices and, inevitably, nepotism - how well the contractor knew the landowner.

A new extractive industry began - an alternative and much more profitable line of work than digging clunch, clay or turf. When the fossil seam was noticed in the Chesterton brick fields in 1848 the owners sold some of what they considered "troublesome annoyances" to Mr. Deck, a Cambridge chemist, for £2 per ton. He probably was not told the royalties the Suffolk manure manufacturers were paying but would have known that similar "phosphatic nodules" were being raised in the Felixstowe and Burwell areas. His tests done on them showed that the Cambridgeshire "coprolites" had between 50% - 60% calcium phosphate, up to 10% higher than the Suffolk variety. It stimulated their extraction as *"a matter of commercial proposition."* (Cambridge Independent Press, 18th January, p.3)

When it was found that the seam extended to the south under Coldham's Common in Barnwell, the industry took off on a large scale. Some Suffolk manure manufacturers and entrepreneurial coprolite contractors, keen to capitalise on the demand, moved into the area to win agreements with brickyard and other landowners to raise the fossils. Gangs of experienced diggers came over to run the Cambridgeshire pits from Suffolk and other counties. (O'Connor, B. (1998), 'The Dinosaurs on Coldham's Common', Bernard O'Connor, Gamlingay) This in-migration was not evidenced in the 1851 census however. There was no reference to fossil or coprolite diggers, coprolite contractors or merchants in any of the parishes where it was then being worked. It is thought that the work was just considered as labouring or, if they were employed by a farmer, as agricultural labour.

It was hardly a coincidence that the geological mapping of the country started around this time. Whilst the exploration was mainly for scientific reasons, knowledge of the extent and distribution of the Greensand was of commercial importance to those who had money to invest in what was to become known as the coprolite diggings.

Averaging about 30 inches thick (about 39cm.), in places the seam was up to six feet (2.1 metres). In some areas it was non-existent, locally called "dead land", due to a slight rise in the seabed whilst the fossils had tended to accumulate in the hollows. Yields therefore varied. In Cambridge itself it was about 300 tons per acre (0.404ha.). In one pit in Wicken it was 2,000 tons but the average was 250 tons per acre. (Kingston, A. (1889) 'Old and New Industries on the Cam.' Warren Press, Royston p.16) When annual agricultural rents were rarely over fifty shillings (£2.50) an acre and these coprolites could be sold at over £2.00 per ton, potentially several hundred pounds could be realised from an acre! Wages of agricultural labourers at that time wouldn't have been over £25 in a year and £200 could have bought a small estate. No wonder there was a lot of interest in them. So began what was termed by the historian, Richard Grove, as "The Cambridgeshire Coprolite Mining Rush". (Oleander Press, Cambridge, 1976)

Throughout the 1850s the seam was worked in

Cambridge. With the development of mass-production in the brick and tile making industry, landowners were able to bring a lot more clay land under cultivation. This was done by laying down drainage tiles. The trenching work for this, or deep ploughing, often revealed the seam a few feet below the surface.

The diggings reached the Ashwell and Hinxworth area in 1857. It was the enclosure and subsequent drainage of Rev. Clutterbuck's land by the surveyor, Bailey Denton, that exposed the coprolite seam. (Clutterbuck, Robert, (1877), 'The Coprolite Beds at Hinxworth', *Trans. Watford Natural History Soc.* Vol. 1. p.238; O'Connor, B. (2000), '*The Ashwell Fossil Diggings*', Bernard O'Connor, Gamlingay) He set up a company to exploit them and his work attracted farmers and manure merchants alike to get involved with the diggings. The fossil deposit was dug from the base of the Lower Cambridgeshire Greensand which outcropped in this area too. Here the coprolite bed was found all round the edge of the chalk marl where it bordered the boulder clay. It lay in a large arc stretching towards St. George's Church and Church Farm in Edworth. Once the landowners realised there was a deposit on their land they would have had it tested and made arrangements for it to be raised, washed and sorted.

The depth and extent of the bed had to be determined. This was done initially by digging a coffin-like pit. A cheaper method was by using a two-man corkscrew borer. Walter Tye, in his account of the Suffolk industry included an interview with one of the diggers who said that

> "To test the depth of the coprolite he made use of a tool like a giant corkscrew, called a 'dipper,' which shuddered in his hands when striking the mineral. Local cottagers always knew what the foreman was after when he came into their gardens carrying his 'dipper.' Naturally, they strongly objected to their gardens being turned topsy-turvy, however much coprolite he might

find there, and they were always delighted to see him go. Old residents today say that a sixpenny tip usually had the desired effect."

Tye, Walter (1930), 'Birth of the Fertilizer Industry', *Fisons Journal*, p.8.)

In places the deposit was found outcropping on the surface but in most cases it had to be dug from between ten and twenty feet (3.7 – 7.4m.) of chalk marl. Where it was found on a small property it was simple matter for the landowner to take on a gang of labourers and have the fossils dug up, washed and sorted and then carted off and sold to a manure manufacturer. In this case it was commonly the farmer's own agricultural labourers. They used to dig the fossils during the low season, once the harvest was in. The work continued over the winter months and then the pits would be left to allow the farm work to start in spring.

If the land was copyhold then the tenant might get permission to raise it using their labourers but occasionally, where a large-scale operation was envisaged, they were evicted and a coprolite manager allowed to move in to the farmhouse. On larger properties an advertisement might be placed in the local press and tenders invited for a contractor to do the work. This occasionally led to existing tenants being given notice to quit to allow the coprolite manager a house to live in whilst the works were in operation but, more often than not, they were compensated for the loss of revenue from those fields which were being dug. Farmers and others set themselves up as coprolite contractors and took on a gang of men and boys. Pick axes, crowbars, shovels, planks, dog irons (supports for the planks), wheelbarrows, trucks and tramway had to be bought and a horse or steam-operated washmill had to be erected to clean the soil and clay from the fossils. A tool shed was erected and another for sorting, having lunch or sheltering from the rain. All this cost money and local bank managers were keen to make loans to enterprising individuals in an industry that had such high returns.

Women and girls were employed in large numbers where the deposit was found in sandier areas. Here the fossils needed sorting to remove any unwanted stones that would reduce the quality and therefore the price paid by the manure manufacturers. There is no census evidence of any female employment in the Arlesey area. The main areas of women and girls being employed in the industry was in the fossil sorting sheds in Wicken in the fens and Potton, near Sandy in Bedfordshire.

Contractors agreed to do the work over a set number of years with them paying the landowner a royalty of so much per ton. The tenant farmer was often compensated for the loss of revenue from those fields out of cultivation by up to £10 an acre. Once work got started the topsoil and subsoil was barrowed to one side of the field to be replaced later. In many cases it was used as the base of the washmill. As the coprolite seam was exposed the diggers shovelled it into wheelbarrows or emptied it into trucks. These were then pushed by hand or pulled by horses along a tramway that ran out of the pit, along the edge of the field or trackway to the washmill. Here their contents were unloaded to create large piles before they were washed and sorted. The soil above the seam on the new face was removed after undercutting, a process which caused considerable danger. Crowbars, pick-axes and shovels were used to make it collapse and, for convenience, it was just thrown into the trench already worked. As shall be seen there were numerous cases of accidents in the pits caused by collapses. This "backfilling" meant that the labourers gradually progressed across the field and onto adjoining property where a new lease was sought. Where another contractor had workings in neighbouring fields pits were opened at opposite ends of the field and two gangs of diggers gradually dug their way towards each other.

The job of washing the fossils got progressively easier over the years. Initially the technique in Suffolk was to dig a trench into the side of the estuary or the river. The actual washing and screening process down at the dock was described in Walter Tye's fascinating insights into the diggings.

> "That was an old man's job when he became too old for the pit. A long tank some thirty feet in length, was specially provided for the job. The coprolites, along with a certain amount of dirt and bones, were shovelled into sieves which, when full, were placed on a ledge in the tank, just under the surface of the water; to each sieve was fastened a long pole, which the washer pulled backwards and forwards until the stones were clean. When there was a shortage of water, in or near the pit, the washing was done at the quayside before loading."

(Tye, W. (1930), op.cit.)

Without access to a tidal estuary, innovative engineers used their skills to develop sophisticated washmills powered by horse or steam engine. A mound was constructed using the top and subsoil. On top of this mound a circular brick base was laid onto which a circular iron tray was placed. Barrow-loads of fossils were wheeled up the mound and emptied into the tray. A pump was often installed to bring the huge quantities of water needed from a nearby water source. Wells sometimes had to be dug and lined with bricks. At one time there were eleven such mills in operation in the Bassingbourn area which were claimed to have been responsible for lowing the water table of the area. (Whitaker, W. (1921), 'Water Supply of Cambs.' *Mem. Geol. Surv.*, London, p.84) A photograph of one of the harrows used can be seen in the illustrations. (Cambridgeshire Collection W27.1. KO. 19554)

The working of these mills was described by the son of the Burwell doctor, Mr Lucas, whose coprolite land was the first to exploited in Cambridgeshire-. Once the coprolite had been brought to the surface: -

Lower Cretaceous Terrestrial Communities
a *Iguanadon* (Vertebrata: Reptilia: Archosaur – dinosaur)
b *Megalosaurus* (Vertebrata: Reptilia: Archosaur – dinosaur)
c *Hypsilophodon* (Vertebrata: Reptilia: Archosaur – dinosaur)
d *Acanthopholis* (Vertebrata: Reptilia: Archosaur – dinosaur)
e *Equisetites* (Pteridophyta: Calamites – horsetails)

(McKerrow, W.S.. (1978), *The Ecology of Fossils: An Illustrated Guide*,
Duckworth, p.297)

The Phosphate bed Community
(McKerrow, W.S.. (1978), *The Ecology of Fossils: An Illustrated Guide*,
Duckworth, p.286)

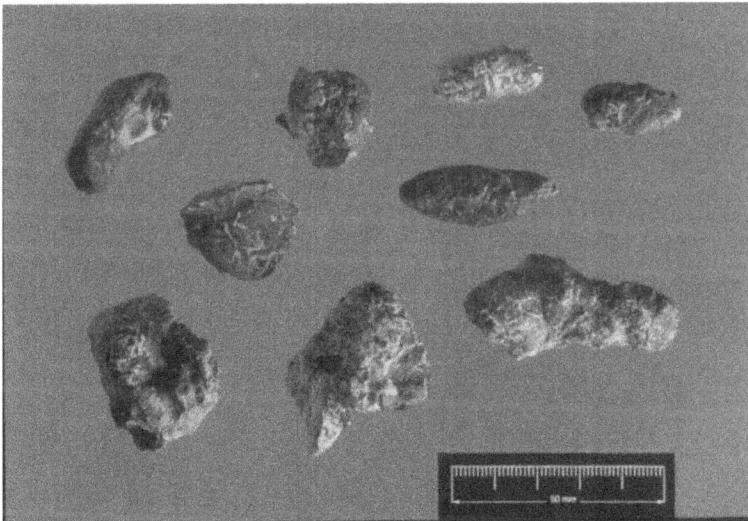

Cambridgeshire coprolites. (Photograph courtesy of Earth
Sciences Museum, Cambridge)

Cambridgeshire coprolites, thought to be 170 million
years old. (Courtesy of Tim Gane)

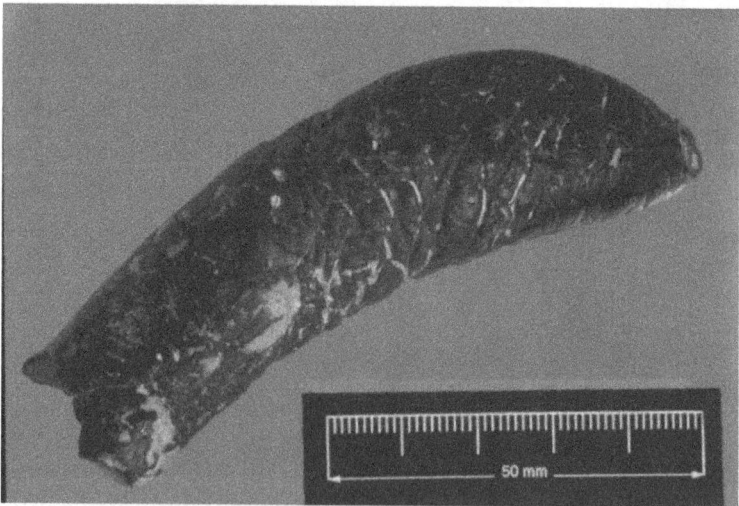

The Barrington coprolite
(Photograph courtesy of Earth Sciences Museum, Cambridge)

The Arlesey Fossil Diggings

North

- • Coprolite workings
- o Location of Coprolite labourers
- ■ Manure Works

Stretham
• Soham
• Wicken
■ BURWELL
• Upware
• Swaffham Prior
Reach • • Swaffham Bulbeck
Cottenham • Bottisham
Westwick • Waterbeach • Lode • Stow-cum-Quy
Horningsea • Milton • Fen Ditton
Chesterton • o Teversham
Madingley • Coton • CAMBRIDGE • Cherry Hinton
Kingston o • Barton Grantchester • Fulbourn
Great Eversden • Comberton • Trumpington
Little Eversden • Haslingfield • Hauxton • Great Shelford
Croydon • Orwell Barrington • Harston • Little Shelford
Wimpole • • Newton
Wrestlingworth • Whaddon • Wendy • Sheprech • o Foxton
Everton • Abington Pigots • McIdreth o Thriplow
Potton • Knapwell • Bassingbourn o Fowlmere
Gamlingay o Litlington DUXFORD
Sutton • Guilden Morden • ROYSTON
Steeple Morden • Ashwell Station
Edworth • Himsworth • Ashwell •
Astwick • Stotfold
Shefford • Henlow
Millbrook • Campton • Arlesey
Ampthill • Clophill • Meppershall • Upper Stondon
Ridgmont Upper • Lower Stondon
Gravenhurst • Shillington
Higham Gobion • • Kirton
• Barton-L-e-Clay

• Brickhill

Leighton Buzzard • Eggington
o • Stanbridge
Billington
o • Slapton • Edlesborough

Dunton Bishopstone
F.1

Coprolite Diggings at Orwell, Cambridgeshire. 1860s – 1870s
(Courtesy of Cambridgeshire Collection W27.1J80 25358)

Coprolite Diggings in Cow Pasture, Abington Pigotts, Cambridgeshire, 1883
(Courtesy of Mr and Mrs Sclater, Abington Pigotts)

Photographs of the coprolite works on Sandy Heath, Bedfordshire, c.1882) The top photo shows women outside the sorting shed. The lower photographs shows a horse-powered cylindrical washmill. (Courtesy of Potton History Society)

Undated photograph of windmills in Bassingbourn, which, once the harvest had been milled, the millstones were replaced with buhr-stones to grind the coprolites. Horse-drawn carts brought the copro-lites along the road from diggings in nearby parishes.

Undated postcard of Bird's manure factory at Duxford, which was used to grind local coprolites and produce superphosphate.

Steam engine hauling coprolites from Whaddon to Shepreth Station c.1880 (Cambridge Collection Q AR J8 11029 Courtesy of Mrs Coningsby, Whaddon

Undated postcard of horse-drawn tumbrils carrying coprolites to the railway station at Millbrook, Bedfordshire.

HORSE-POWERED COPROLITE WASHMILL

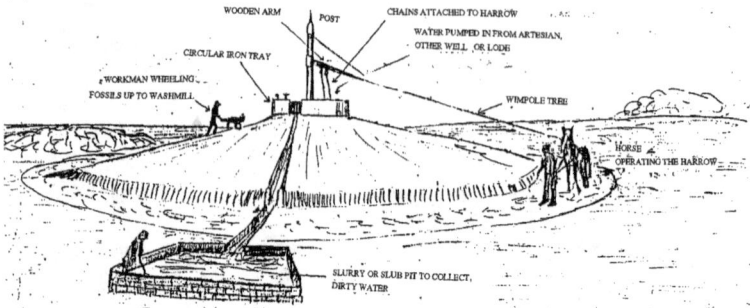

(Based on sketch in Richard Grove's Cambridgeshire Coprolite Mining Rush)

Undated photograph of a circular coprolite harrow
Cambridgeshire Collection: W27.1. KO. 19554).

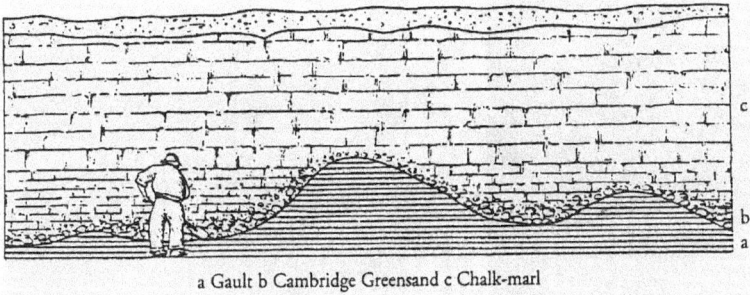

a Gault b Cambridge Greensand c Chalk-marl

View of a coprolite pit in Horningsea, Cambs.
(Jukes-Browne, A.J. & Hill, W. *Cretaceous Rocks of Britain,* Mem. Geol. Surv. 1903, p.194)

Undated photograph of coprolite diggers in Orwell, Cambridgeshire
(Courtesy of Sue Miller, Orwell History Society)

Photographs of the coprolite works on Sandy Heath, Bedfordshire, c.1882) The top photo shows women outside the sorting shed. The lower photographs shows a horse-powered cylindrical washmill. (Courtesy of Potton History Society)

Caricature of J.B. Lawes who patented the technique of dissolving coprolite and other phosphatic materials in sulphuric acid to produce superphosphate. He set up his own manure company, won contracts to raise coprolites and purchased others from diggings across south-east England (*Vanity Fair* 8th July 1882)

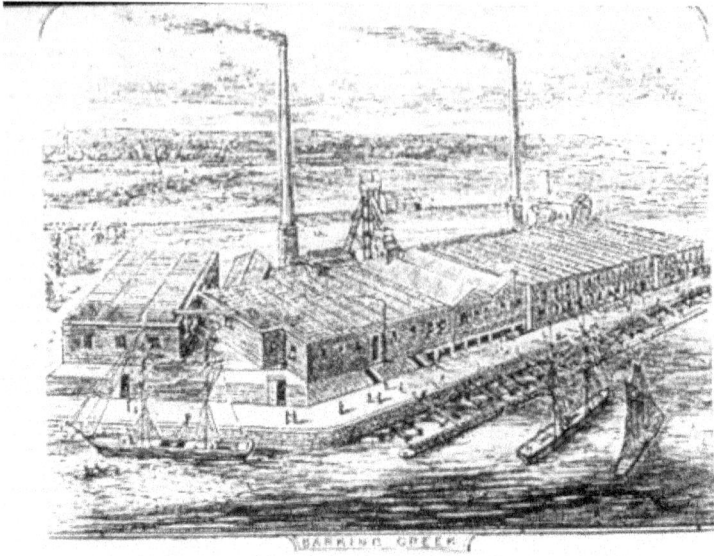

BARKING CREEK.

LAWES' MANURE FACTORY, DEPTFORD CREEK.

(Courtesy of Lawes Agricultural Trust, Rothamsted Agricultural Station)

Undated photograph of coprolites being unloaded at Lawes'
Chemical Manure Works at Barking, London
(Courtesy of Rural History Centre, Reading University Neg. No.
35/23594)

R. & H. WALTON,

MANUFACTURERS OF ALL KINDS OF

MANURES,

EAST ROAD, AND COLDHAM ROAD,
CAMBRIDGE.

Blood Manure, Corn Manure, Turnip Manure, Mangold Manure,
SUPERPHOSPHATE OF LIME,
PREPARED NIGHT SOIL FOR CORN.

The following articles supplied in any quantity for mixing purposes:—

Half Inch Bones; Quarter Inch Bones; Sulphuric Acid;
Muriatic Acid; Sulphate of Ammonia; Agricultural Salt;
Soot; &c., &c.

Experienced Men sent out for mixing if required.

BONE AND MANURE WORKS,
EAST ROAD, AND COLDHAM ROAD, CAMBRIDGE.

Robert Walton's advert, Kelly's Post Office Directory 1864

Undated photograph of Edward Packard (1819 – 1899) who founded Edward Packard and Company. In 1843 he began making super-phosphate by dissolving old bones in sulphuric acid at Snape Mill. In 1851 he built Britain's first complete sulphuric acid and superphosphate works at Bramford and went on to win coprolite agreements and pur-chase coprolites from across southeast England.
(http://www.yara.com/en/about/yara_centennial/heritage/
fisons_inter.html)

1861 photograph of William Colchester (1813–1898), one of the first manure manufacturers to use Suffolk coprolites. Had manure works in Ipswich, moved into Cambridgeshire fens in 1846, won coprolite contracts and purchased others from diggings across southeast England.
(Courtesy of Giles Colchester)

Coprolite workings at Brickhill in 1880s (Arthur Bates, Aylesbury Museum)

Photograph c.1870s of phosphate mining in Charleston, South Carolina (Unknown source)

Extract from 1-inch geological map sheet 46, mapped in 1884 by
A.Jukes-Browne showing the Shillington
coprolite works

Distribution of the Greensand and Gault Clay in Bedfordshire

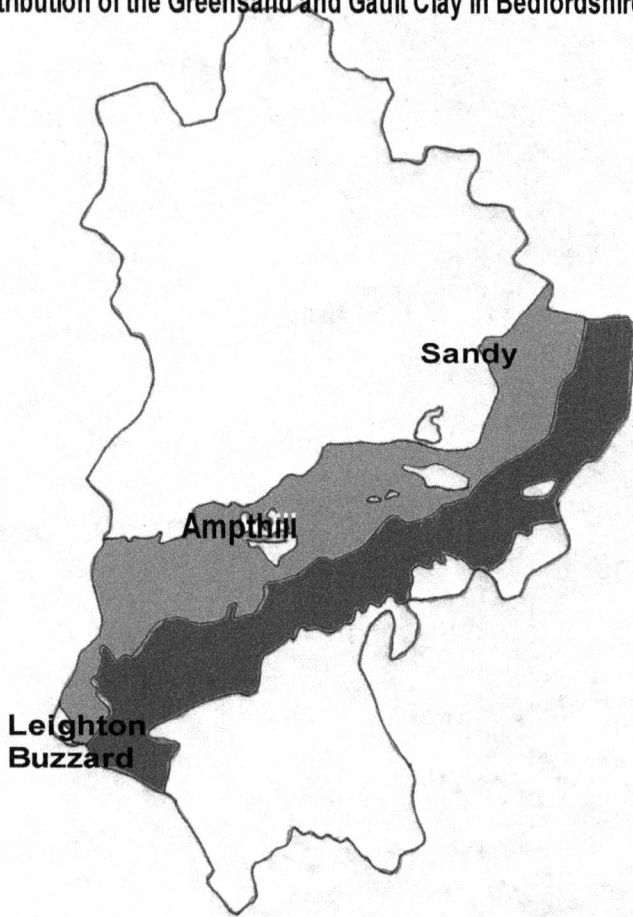

Sandy

Ampthill

Leighton
Buzzard

Scale not exact

Distribution of Bedfordshire's Coprolite Parishes

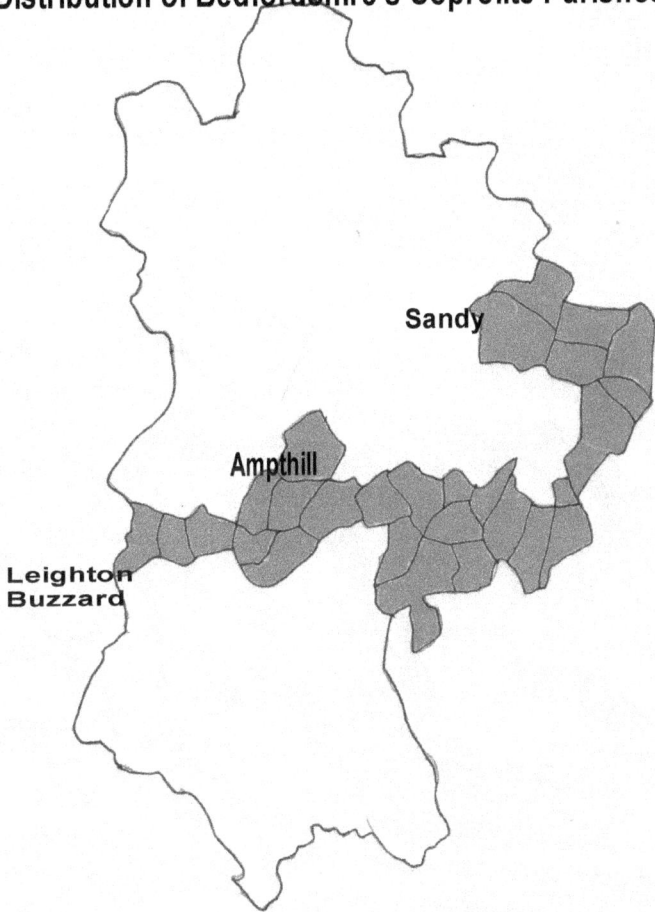

Sandy

Ampthill

Leighton
Buzzard

Scale not exact

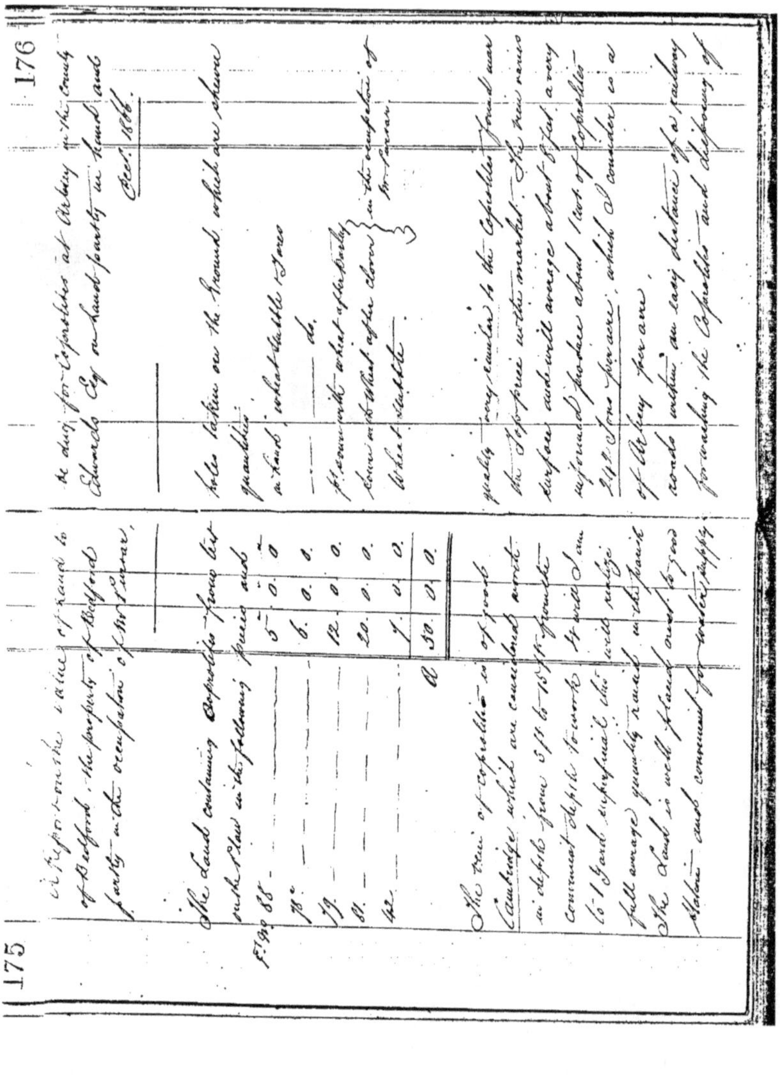

175

A Report on the Value of Land to
of Bedford, the property of Bedford
partly in the occupation of Mr Purser,

The Land containing Coprolites from test
on the Plan in the following pieces and

F.t No 88		5	0	0
78		6	0	0
79		12	0	0
81		20	0	0
42		7	0	0
	A	50	0	0

The vein of coprolites is of good
Cambridge which are considered worth
in depth from 5 ft to 15 ft from the
convenient depth to work. It will I am
to 1 Yard superficial this will realize
full average quantity raised in the parish
The Land is well placed next to good
Station and convenient for water supply.

176

be dug for Coprolites at Arlsey in the County
Edwards Esq on Land partly in hand and
Decr. 1866.

holes taken on the Ground which are shewn
quantities:
in hand, wheat stubble & Tares
do.
pt. sown with wheat after barley
sown with Wheat after clover } in the occupation of Mr Purser
Wheat stubble.

quality very similar to the Coprolites found near
the Top price in the market. The vein varies
surface and will average about 8 feet a very
uniform and produce about 1 cwt. of Coprolites
242 Tons per acre, which I consider is a
of Arlsey per acre.
roads within an easy distance of a railway
for washing the Coprolites and disposing of

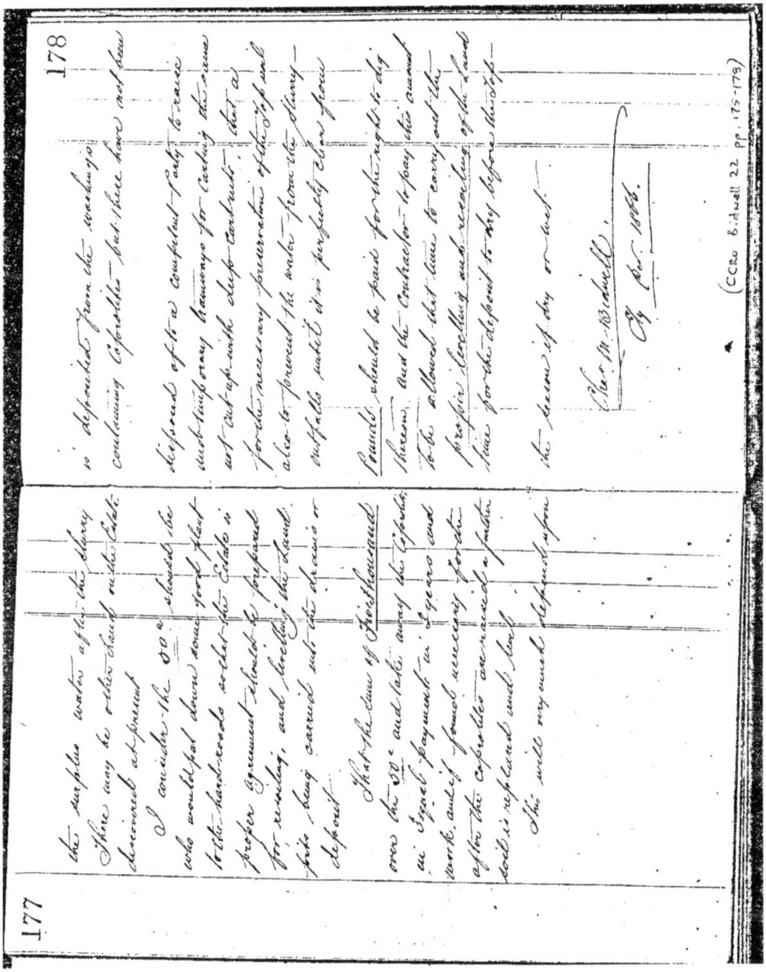

178

177

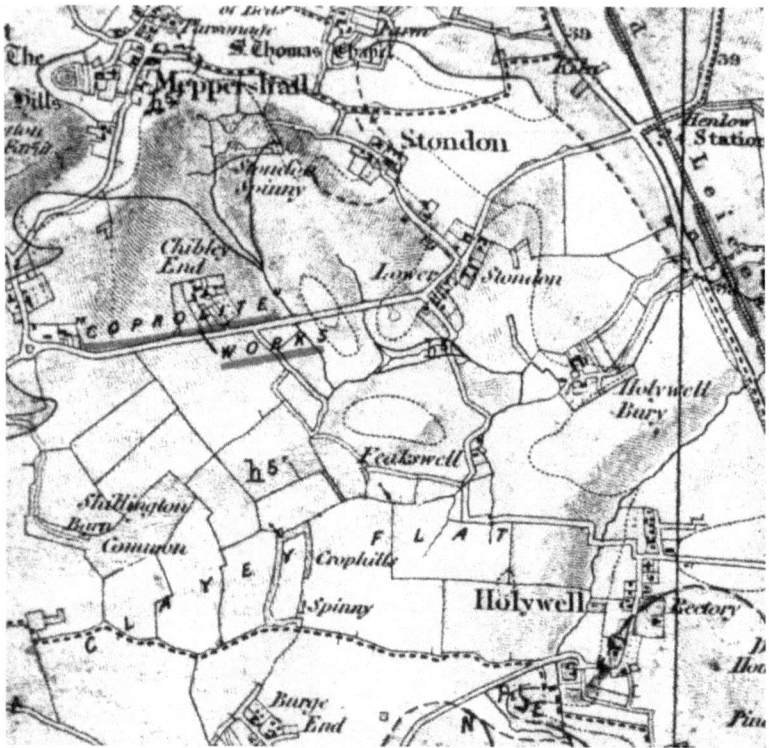

Extract from First Edition 1864 Geological map of Bedfordshire showing coprolite works between Stondon and Shillington

The Accident at Arlesey Sidings Station. 23rd December 1876

(BCRO. Photograph ref. Z50/2/4).

Phosphate mill at Charleston Mining Company's works
(Frank Leslie's Illustrated Newspaper June 30th 1877)

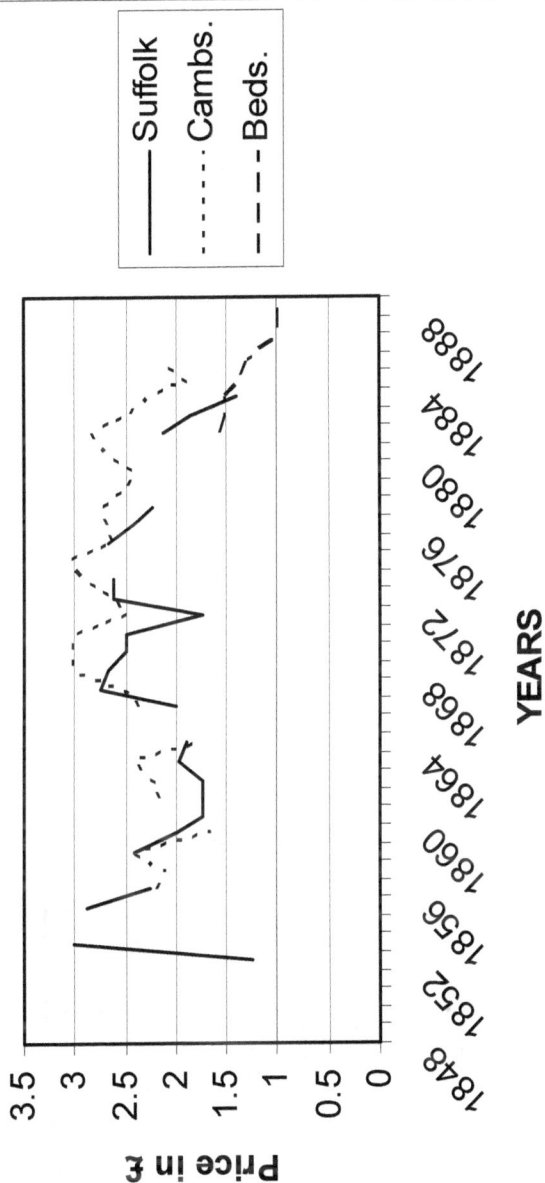

Fluctuations in Coprolite Sale Prices

Legend:
— Suffolk
······ Cambs.
– – Beds.

Price in £: 3.5, 3, 2.5, 2, 1.5, 1, 0.5, 0

YEARS: 1848, 1852, 1856, 1860, 1864, 1868, 1872, 1876, 1880, 1884, 1888

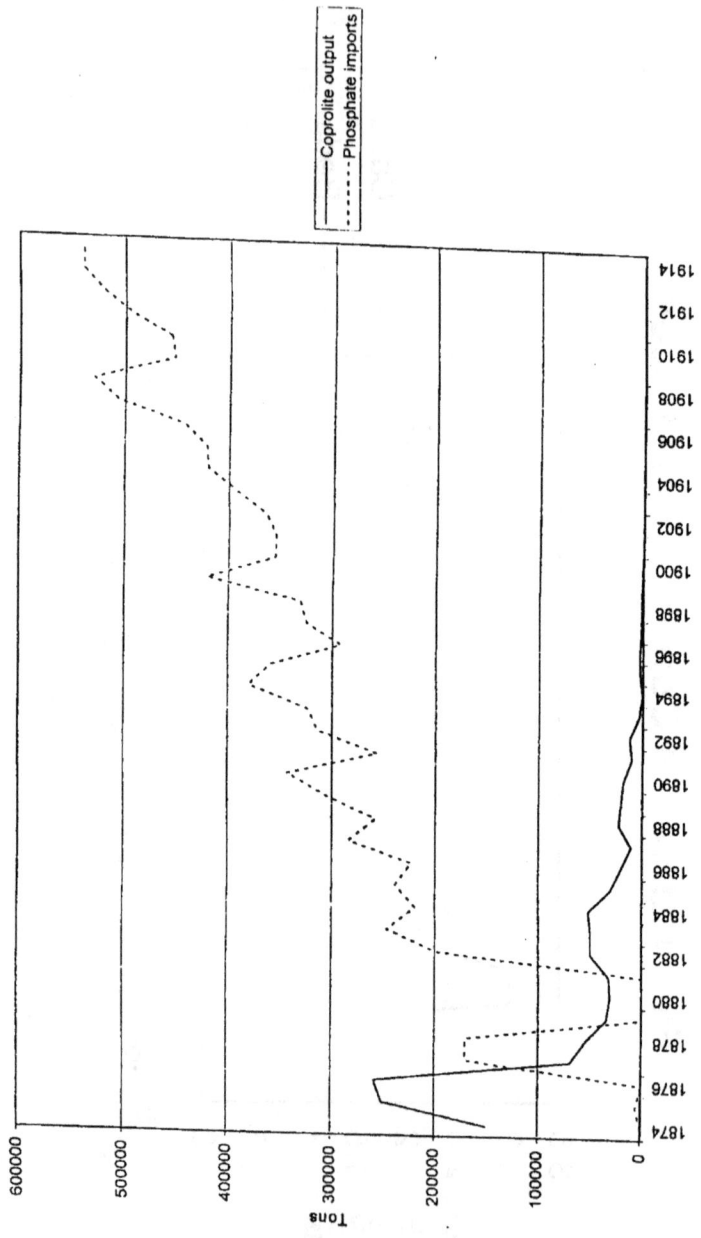

Coprolite Production and Phosphate Imports 1874-1914

Legend:
— Coprolite output
---- Phosphate imports

"The first thing to do was to throw up a hill in the middle of the ground, and this was done by first erecting- a post about ten or twelve feet long, and throwing the soil around it to a height of eleven or twelve feet and of thirty feet in diameter. Three feet from the centre a ring would be formed six to eight feet wide and four feet deep. This would be paved with bricks and the sides would be sheets of iron. On one side of the hill a platform was made from a wooden tank, to which was connected a pump eighteen feet long; a pipe from the tank would go with the ring and opposite the tank was a trapped outlet, and on the outer side of the hill a square of about two chains would be earthed up a little to form a sort of pan. From the central post a wooden arm would be attached about twelve to fourteen feet long; to this would be attached a wimpole tree, to which a horse would be yoked. Connected to the centre of the post would be a light rail which was fixed to the horse bridle to keep the horse always in is track; from the arm would be suspended two iron harrows which ran well in on the bottom of the ring. When the soil containing the fossils was wheeled up to the ring a sufficient quantity of water would be let in. As the horse went round a creamy fluid would be produced and the fossils would drop on the floor. Then the trapped outlet would be opened and the creamlike fluid, called "slurry" would flow into pans. This operation having been repeated a number of times the fossils on the floor would be washed clear of earth and weighed up".

(Lucas, C. (1930), op.cit. p.31)

The cost of constructing these mills in the late-1840s when they were first developed was £100 but by 1875 the *"coprolite contractors had become so expeditious that a hill could be put up for £5!* (Ibid.) In some areas a less expensive but more efficient process was developed. This was a cylindrical wash mill, rather like an early version of today's vegetable washer. They were in use over in Potton where they were described in an article in the Bedfordshire Times.

> "... the coprolites are wheeled in barrows to another portion of the ground where a cylindrical sieve is fixed for the purpose of freeing them from the sand. This machine, which is worked by horsepower, is a round cylinder of sheet iron, perforated with holes of a quarter inch diameter and placed horizontally in a tank of water, the cylinder being half submerged. The drum of the cylinder is two ft. in diameter at the larger end and 1 ft. at the smaller and 10 ft. in length.
>
> The fossils are put in at the larger end, and as the drum revolves the smallest stones and the sand fall through the holes into the water tank, and the larger are carried along by a screw arrangement, and emptied at the smaller end into barrows. When these are filled they are wheeled by men into the sorting sheds where women are engaged in sorting. These sheds, 28 ft. long by 8 ft. wide, have on each side a bench, separated by partitions with room for one woman to work.
>
> The fossils being largely mixed with sandstones, it is necessary that they should be removed before they are ready for market. The fossils in their mixed state, are emptied on the benches and sorted, the stones being thrown onto the floor and the fossils passed through a hole at the back of the benches into a box outside. They are then wheeled into heaps ready for sale.

(Bedfordshire Times, May 18th 1962. from an original article in 1878)

Some of the local contractors and farmers would have used this method. Yet another technique was employed in Hinxworth, just over the border in Hertfordshire. Audrey Kiln's research into the industry involved interviewing some of the old diggers. Mr Street told her about the washing process in Hinxworth Barns. face they were shovelled into carts and taken by horse to be washed in "Hinxworth Barns".

> *"The eaves in the barn he estimated at 20 feet high. Housed in the barn was a portable steam engine, fired by wood and coal, which was connected by a belt to a huge wooden wheel which Mr Street said missed the roof by inches. Underneath the wheel was a large washing trough. The wheel had large metal cups attached to each strut. The fossils were placed into the trough and water was let in through a pipe. The wheel was driven by the engine and as the cups passed through the trough they picked up the fossils, carried them round, and replaced them in clean water at the bottom of the trough. The slurry was then released from the trough by removing a large plug. Until recent years, part of the wheel could be seen standing outside The Barn, but unfortunately there is no record of its existence now."*

> (Kiln, A. (1969), *'The Coprolite Industry'*, Thesis for Putteridge Bury College, p. 32)

As the technology improved, steam powered washmills were introduced by those contractors who could afford it. After several such washings the dirty water, locally termed "slub" or "slurry" was run back into "slurry pans" to dry out before the topsoil was replaced. The theory was that once dried the cracks in it would allow better drainage. As the work progressed across the field the mill was transferred to a more accessible site. The topsoil was barrowed back into the trench or slurry pit and levelled ready for cultivation. Whilst the theory was that this process would improve the soil, in practise the operation was not always done thoroughly. It was cheaper for a contractor to cover it up quickly and move on.

A farmer, however, would take care as he would benefit from improved cropping. In several areas white chalk markings can still be seen on the fields which indicate where slurry was not properly covered or the topsoil replaced. Astute land agents ensured that agreements included very precise instructions for this process and subsequent drainage, levelling and seeding.

From Hinxworth it was about a two-mile journey for the tumbrils of coprolites to be taken to Arlesey Station. Business for local carters must have been good as there are documented coprolite workings in Astwick, Edworth, Hinxworth, Ashwell, Stotfold, Henlow, Hinxworth, Stondon, Shefford, Shillington and Meppershall. Loaded into drop-sided trucks the coprolites would then have been sent to the manure factories of Cambridge, Ipswich, London and elsewhere. Horses would have been a common sight hauling tumbrils loaded with washed coprolites along the country lanes to Arlesey station on the Great Northern Railway. Some went to Baldock or Ashwell stations. From here railway trucks would take them to manure factories in Ipswich, London and elsewhere. Some would have been taken into Cambridge to the wharf by Silver Street bridge. A barge or fenland lighter would take them up the Cam and Ouse to King's Lynn for transhipment round the coast. Others were carted direct to local bone mills like Walton's on East Road, Cambridge or the Cambridge Manure Company's works on Histon Road. This company was set up in the early-1850s by the Cambridge auctioneer, John Rolfe Mann, a Fulbourn merchant, A. P. Chaplin, and other "agriculturalists" and entrepreneurs who recognised the profits to be made in this lucrative business. The Cambridge solicitor, Clement Francis, was to act as their "undisclosed agent." (Cambridge Collection (CC) Cooper's Misc. Papers, 32. 1856; CCRO Francis & Co. Bill Books, 1855 pp.455,539; CCRO R60/3 Cambridge Manure Co. Minute Books.) Many local bone and corn mills had to be converted as the gritstone was not hard enough to grind the coprolites. A hard buhrstone had to be installed in its place. Herbert Fordham's corn mill in Odsey, near Ashwell was changed so that he could add value to the coprolites he was raising locally..

With "super" being sold at up to £7 a ton, half the price of guano, it became much in demand across the country. It was not long therefore before sales were being promoted across Europe, in America and throughout the Empire. There were reports of sales as far afield as Russia and Queensland. During the 1850s there were four manure factories in Cambridge. With them paying an average forty-three shillings and sixpence (£2.18) a ton in 1856 for Cambridge coprolites there were profits to be made by coprolite contractors and merchants. The deposit had been mapped in most of the Eastern Counties by the 1870s. Although the two seams ere not continuous, the Greensand fossils were worked from parts of Suffolk, Norfolk, Cambridgeshire, Hertfordshire, Bedfordshire, Buckinghamshire, Oxfordshire, Hampshire, Yorkshire and Kent. Similar deposits were also worked in France and Belgium. Its enormous extent allowed many new manure companies to capitalise on this new raw material and take a share of the increasing market for artificial fertilisers. Accordingly, many new chemical manure works were opened on the coprolite belt in Burwell, Duxford, Shepreth, Royston, Bassingbourn and Odsey near Ashwell.

One of Cambridge's iron founders, James Ind Headley, who built the famous Eagle steam engine, was very much involved in the coprolite business. He had his own coprolite works erected behind his Eagle Foundry on Mill Road in Cambridge and had his works, "*well fitted up to make the pumps, washmills, cast iron screens and steam engines to provide power.*" (Enid Porter's notebooks Cambridge Folk Museum 15/64-65) He was aware of the investment opportunities in this area and luck had it that one of his relatives lived in Coton whose land was dug for coprolites. In the early-1850s coprolite contractors were paying landowners royalties of between seven and fifteen shillings a ton for all the coprolites they raised. This entailed having a weighbridge set up by the works and for accurate measurements to be recorded. To avoid errors and dependence on the contractors' weighings the land agents suggested an alternative scheme whereby royalties should be paid according to how many acres were dug over the year. This entailed having the pits surveyed around Lady Day (May

1st) and Michaelmas (September 29th). The surveyor's measurements could then be used to determine how much the contractor owed. This provided local businesses like Bidwell, Francis, Smith, Carter Jonas and Mann and Raven a valuable additional source of income for the next forty years. Royalties ranged from as high as £400 to as low as £30 an acre but the average was about £100. This was about forty to fifty times the revenue the landowners could get from agricultural rents. After labour and other costs were deducted the contractors could make a big profit.

There was no evidence in the 1861 census of anyone in this area being described as involved in the diggings. That is not to say that there were none. Maybe the work was considered as agricultural labour. As it tended on small-scale operations to be practised over the winter months maybe those engaged in the work were back on farm work. If gangs of outsiders had moved in it is unlikely they would have stayed around when they knew a government census was to be taken. Maybe the census enumerator did not recognise the word coprolite and simply described it as general labour. Local gossip has it that gangs of Irish labourers were involved in the diggings but documentary evidence of this has not emerged.

An analysis of the census returns shows significant population increases in the local parishes over the decade to 1861. Overall there was a 17% increase. Whilst the coming of the railway was the major reason for the increase, the availability of coprolite labour can not be claimed to be a factor.

Coprolite Villages	1851	1861
Astwick	81	64
Dunton	467	518
Edworth	104	99
Eyeworth	141	149
Langford	986	1086
Arlesey	1095	1401
Campton	548	529

Shefford	1052	1015
Clifton	1053	1478
Henlow	970	1011
Meppershall	503	541
Shefford Hardwick	63	56
Shitlington	1598	1788
Upper Stondon	46	66
Stotfold	1395	2071
Total	10102	11872

The coprolite works started in Shillington, about four miles to the west of Arlesey, just after the census in 1862. One of the landowners, William Wilshere, arranged with Mr Lawes to have them raised from Chibley Farm, where the seam had been found during drainage operations. Wilshere's neighbour, Robert Long, who farmed Manor Farm in Stondon noted in his journal of 28th June that year that "*At Chibley Farm which is adjoining ours they have this week begun to dig out Coprolites for the manufacture of Turnip manure.*" (BCRO.X159/3) After washing and sorting the coprolites were carted to the railway station at Henlow. From here they then taken in low-sided wagons to Lawes' chemical manure works at Barking. Lawes employed George Beaver, a surveyor from Hitchin, to undertake borings and measurements at the works. Insight into the undertaking has come from his diary,

"Friday 1st August 1862, I begin works connected with coprolite diggings, just lately commenced by the agents of Mr John Bennet Lawes of Rothamsted, Harpenden, on Chibley Farm, Shillington, the estate of Wm. Wilshere Esq., Mr George Lines being the tenant thereof. And on Saturday, the 2nd instant, I journey to the works at Chibley and have an interview with Mr Wyatt, the manager for Mr. Lawes - this being the commencement of a long engagement and connection of business."

(George Beaver's diaries, Hitchin Museum, p.73a)

Wyatt engaged a gang of able-bodied men. Whether they were from outside the area of local labourers is unknown. The success of the operation led to tests being done on Manor Farm in Stondon. Robert Long's journal noted that on 13th September the same year *"Coproilite prospectors doing trial diggings."* (BCRO.X159/3; Communication with David Cooper, Shefford) These must have been Beaver's men. The diggings extended along the foot of the slope into Stondon parish. There are reports of them being in full operation by 1870. (Hitchin Museum, G. Beaver's diary p.93a; 1st Ed. 6" Geological map, Beds)

Beaver took measurements of the pits twice a year, around Lady Day and Michaelmas, to determine the amount of royalty that had to be paid to the landowner. His diary had several entries about his visits to Stondon but gave no indication of the financial arrangements. Lawes' royalties in Shillington were up to £130 per acre but documentation of his agreements in Stondon have not come to light. The larger landowners engaged land agents to supervise their estates and some of their correspondence, surveyors' notebooks and agreements have been deposited in the local Record Offices. Documentation of agreements with the smaller landowners has generally been lost. However, the records that do exist shed interesting light on the development of the industry in this area.

At Michaelmas 1862 Lawes moved into the Astwick area. With his competitors having a strong foothold in the Cambridge area he was keen to dominate this area of newly discovered coprolites in Bedfordshire. He leased 10 acres, part of a field called Fox Holes, owned by Charles Cholmerley Hale. It was tenanted by Hugh Fossey Smyth. There was no indication as to how much royalty per acre Lawes paid. Like the land in Hinxworth and Ashwell it

"...had been drained in 1855 at the expense of the tenant, (less the tiles). In the Spring of 1862 was all

manured with good dung and 2 cwts. of Lawes' manure
per acre for turnips which is a good preparation for a
succession of crops."

(Document in possession of Mr D. Smyth, Edworth)

Mr. Smyth was given notice to quit in 1863 and was eventually compensated with £138 5 0d. Who Mr. Lawes engaged to supervise the workings and arrange the transport of the washed fossils to Arlesey station is unknown. It could have been Mr Wyatt, his coprolite manager at Shillington. The work entailed raising these fossils would have provided fairly lucrative employment for many local men and boys. It even attracted men from outside the area. This inward migration will be referred to later. Mr Farey, a local man, told of how, from Foxholes, the work progressed generally eastwards through Great Mead, Little Mead, Thorns, part at the top of 30 Acres, Sward Brook and 18 Acres towards Hinxworth. The seam was also found on Old Farm, 6 Acres in the ditch, east of Glebe Farm and just south of Hinxworth. In all likelihood all these fields would have been worked. (Ibid.)

To allow easier access for the traffic along the Great North Road over the top of Topler's Hill a cutting had been made. Here the gault clay met the chalk marl in Astwick Field and the coprolite bed was exposed in the Greensand formation. A coprolite pit on the west side of the road, just below the top, was marked on a subsequent geological map of the area. (O.S. 6 inch Beds. 23NE 1931) Drivers today coming south on the Al are probably completely unaware that the fields on both sides of the road down to the Tudor Oaks Public House would have been the scene of large scale open cast mining last century.

Jack Wilson of Edworth, worked in the diggings and was able to retire on the money he had made. He lived happily on his four acres keeping a few pigeons. In Astwick field, he had said, there was a wooden paymaster's shack where the coprolite gang were paid and the fossils were washed in

Hinxworth Field Barns which used to be thatched. A little track ran down Love's Farm from the "quarries" to these barns and beyond Jarmans there were white patches in the fields where the subsoil had been brought to the surface and the men had not replaced the topsoil. "Slub pans" were also to be found near these patches where the wastewater from the washing of the coprolites was allowed to accumulate and dry out before supposedly being put on the diggings before the topsoil was replaced. In the Middle of Saltmore there was a well and a ring of bricks which was another site of the washmill. (Author's communication with Mr D. Smyth, Edworth)

Working conditions in the pits varied according to the season. The busiest time of year was from the autumn to the last winter frosts. Audrey Kiln reported an interview she had with a Mr Street from Hinxworth, who described the spades they used.

> "...the shaft was of metal, about two foot long and a wooden T-shaped handle, about 5 inches wide, was fixed into the top of this. The blade was narrow, the top being about four inches, narrowing to 2 inches, with an overall length of 6 inches."

(Kiln. op.cit. pp.43-4)

Mr Street started coprolite work with his father when he was only ten and his task was to sort out the washed stones and remove such items as stones or pebbles unacceptable by the manure manufacturers. He claimed that women and girls were also engaged to do this sorting for what was the comparatively low wages of only three shillings (£0.15) a week.

> "To avoid cutting their hands on the sharp-edged shells they used a wooden scraper to push the coprolites from side to side. Refuse was thrown over their shoulders and any items of interest, such as sharks' teeth, were collected and sold to supplement their earnings."

(Ibid.p.38)

The census returns did not mention any female involvement in local parishes. It may have been that they had returned to farm work in the spring. Many diggers started in their youth on basic digging work and, in time, progressed through other aspects of the work to become quite experienced. A great deal of heavy labour was involved in digging trenches to reach the seam but occasionally the fossils were scattered within the subsoil which necessitated additional work. William Sale, remembered when he was

"...transferred to the job of sifting and carrying away the earth removed by the diggers. It was customary to have young lads working at the bottom of the trenches in order to handle this work, part of which involved loading and carrying a three stone tin of fossils up the planks to the pit top for removal to the washing mill. He was twelve, and his wages had been increased to the munificent sum of 5/- per week...

The boys worked in pairs, one pair to a digger and they were kept very busy. Their day started at 8am. and they finished for the evening at 6pm. They were allowed half an hour for lunch and worked a six-day-week. Referring to those times as "the good old days", he said that had he been working on the land, his average wage would have been 2/- per day. When one realises that at that time the national average wage for adult men engaged in agriculture was 8/- to 10/- per week, it is little wonder that the local men preferred to work the pits than the land.

On wet days, the boys practised walking the planks, imitating the skilled barrow runners and preparing for the time when, as adults, they would take their place as runners. The less experienced men usually started working at the bottom 'kench', where there was little fear of falling from the planks when the soil was being shifted. As the men gained more experience they were promoted to higher 'kenches', where the work was obviously more risky. The layers of coprolite were dug out by shovel or crowbar and care had to be taken to watch the sides of the trenches for cracks. Mr Street said that collapses were fairly frequent and sometimes men became trapped beneath fallen earth. It was customary to have a man standing on the top of the trench watching the sides, ready to shout a warning to those below at the first sign of trouble. The depth of the pits varied from as little as 12 feet, but 20 feet was considered about the normal depth both for the safety of the men and for the economics involved.

Mr Sale told of the horseplay that used to go on among the more experienced diggers, much to the consternation of those below apparently. "I was told of men who actually stood on their heads on the uppermost planks and of one man who actually used to cartwheel along the length of the top plank. Mr Street couldn't remember an incidence of a barrow falling off."

(Kiln, op.cit. pp.40-41)

It would appear that these gymnasts were not confined to the this area. Walter Tye, in his study of the Suffolk workings, mentions men who were "*reputed to have stood on their heads on the topmost plank. This explains their keenness for joining the Navy after the pits were closed.*" (Tye, W. (1930), op.cit. p.7) Sale went on to say that

"Inspection of the planks each morning was routine, usually undertaken by the foreman but, if he was not available, then by the most experienced diggers. On cold or frosty mornings it was usual to turn the planks and fasten them very securely before commencing to use them as "roads."

...Planks were also tested for flexibility. Taut boards were considered unsafe and were not used by the copperliters. Sometimes a loud crack announced a plank failure and the men on the bottom dived for cover. The carriers quickly accustomed their bodyweight to the bend and whip of the planks they were walking over with their loads and walked with the ease of men traversing solid road surfaces. I was told,

however, that those working below always kept a wary eye open whenever the boards were being walked.

As the diggers reached the bottom of the seam, water started seeping in and working became very uncomfortable. Black sand, oozing with black water, quickly soaked through even the thickest boot and froze the workmen's feet, also making them very sore. It was often necessary to lay a pipe in the bottom of the pit in an attempt to drain off the water. Below a certain depth, however, this was not possible because the water dripped from all sides into the trench. Mr Sale also spoke of a small engine-driven pump sometimes used by the copperliters. This was portable and fired with wood or coal."

(Kiln, op.cit.pp.41-4)

They had used their ingenuity too by developing a barrow with a bigger front wheel. This allowed them to see where it was on the plank and avoid a fall. Once the fossils in Hinxworth had been barrowed to the surface they were shovelled into carts and taken by horse to be washed in "Hinxworth Barns". Mr Street described the process.

"The eaves in the barn he estimated at 20 feet high. Housed in the barn was a portable steam engine, fired by wood and coal, which was connected by a belt to a huge wooden wheel which Mr Street said missed the roof by inches. Underneath the wheel was a large washing trough. The wheel had large metal cups attached to each strut. The fossils were placed into the trough and water was let in through a pipe. The wheel was driven by the engine and as the cups passed through the trough they picked up the fossils, carried them round, and replaced them in clean water at the bottom of the trough. The slurry was then released from the trough by removing a large plug. Until recent years, part of the wheel could be seen standing outside The Barn, but unfortunately there is no record of its existence now."

(Ibid.p.32)

More than likely this and other metal remnants of the industry would have been made in William Colchester's Bassingbourn Iron Works. This supplied many of the local coprolite contractors with equipment. It could have been sold back as scrap when the industry came to a halt. There are reports that some contractors in financial difficulties simply buried their plant and machinery in their pit.

By the mid-1860s the land agents called in by landowners to arrange the coprolite contracts altered the arrangements. Instead of a royalty being paid for every ton raised which incurred difficulties in accurate weighing at the site, it was recommended that royalties per acre were paid. As this entailed taking accurate surveys twice a year it provided the surveyors with a regular source of income. Lawes took on the services of the Hitchin-based surveyor, George Beaver, who recorded in his diary

> "On the 3rd Jan.1863 I go to Edworth to make survey of some lands for coprolite diggings on the estate of Mr. Hale of King's Walden - this is the commencement of works in that quarter."

> (Beaver's diaries, Hitchin Museum, p.74a)

Lawes gained permission from Charles Cholmerly Hale to work one of his fields on Edworth Bury Farm.

The earliest documentary evidence of coprolite digging in Arlesey was in October 1866, the same year that the Arlesey Siding was completed. Although no documentation has emerged to confirm it, having a railway so close to the works were to prove a significant advantage. Bedford Edwards, one of the local landowners, invited Charles Bidwell, an experienced coprolite surveyor from Ely to value some fields being farmed by Mr Pursar, his tenant farmer. They were Nos. 42, 78, 79, 81, 88 on the Arlesey enclosure map *"on land partly in hand and partly in the occupation of Mr Pursar."* Mr. Bidwell's report proved exceedingly welcome. It foretold a massive increase to Edwards' usual income. It indicated that they were already being worked in nearby fields. Who was responsible for the original operation is uncertain but it was probably John Lawes of Rothamsted.

"The vein of coprolites is of good quality very similar to the Coprolites found near Cambridge which are considered worth the top price in the market. The vein varies in depth from 3ft. to 15ft. from the surface and will average about 8 feet, a very convenient depth to work. It will, I am informed, produce about 1 cwt. of Coprolites to 1 Yard superficial. This will realise 242 Tons per acre, which I consider is a full average quantity raised in the parish of Arlesey per acre.

The land is well placed next to good roads within an easy distance of a railway Station and convenient for water supply or washing the Coprolites and disposing of the surplus water after the slurry is deposited from the washings. There may be other land on the Estate containing coprolite but these have not been discovered at present.

I consider the 50 acres should be disposed of to a competent party to Raise who would put down some good plant and temporary tramways for carting the same to the hard-roads so that the Estate is not cut up with deep cart ruts, that a proper agreement should be prepared for the necessary preservation of the topsoil for resoiling, and levelling the land also to prevent the water from the slurry-pits being carried into the drains or outfalls until it is perfectly clean from deposit.

That the sum of Five Thousand Pounds should be paid for the right to dig over the 50 acres and take away the coprolites thereon and the contractor to pay this amount in 3 equal payments in 3 years and to be allowed that time to carry out the work and, if found necessary for the proper levelling and resoiling of the land after the coprolites are raised, a further time for the deposit to dry before the top soil is replaced and level.

This will very much depend on the season if dry or wet."

(CCRO. 515/Bidwell's Valuation Book 21; Bidwell 22 pp.175-8)

£5,000 was an immense fortune in those days. Agricultural rents rarely reached £1.50 an acre and an agricultural labourer might only expect £25 a year! What Edwards spent this additional revenue on is not known? (CCRO. Bidwell's 1868 diary 3rd March) The Earl of Hardwick at Wimpole Hall was reported to be making £5,000 a year from his coprolite royalties. Such a sum would have meant a coprolite contractor of considerable means would have had to take on the operation. Mr. Bidwell's survey of the works in March the following year did not mention the name of the contractor but subsequent evidence shows that a lease for the fifty acres went to John Bennet Lawes, the Rothamsted landowner, agriculturalist and manurial entrepreneur.

Mr. Lawes had patented the method of dissolving phosphates in sulphuric acid in 1842 to make "super". Buying the fossils from some farmers at less than a £1.00 a ton and selling the manure at up to £7.00 a ton meant big profit margins. He also received £0.25 royalty for every ton of super made by other manufacturers. With two manure works on the Thames in London and many coprolite contracts across Cambridgeshire and Suffolk he was well on his way to amassing a personal fortune. He already had a foothold in Bedfordshire working the pits in and around Shillington from 1862. (O'Connor, B. (1990), 'Rothamsted, Lawes and Dinosaurs', unpublished work; Whitaker, W. and Skertchley (1891) 'The Geology of parts of Cambridge and of Suffolk', *Mem.Geol.Surv.*)

Although no evidence of his lease with a landowner has emerge d, Mr. Lawes would have taken on a foreman and a large number of men and boys. In many coprolite parishes, hoards of "strangers" descended on the coprolite workings. Fascinating insight into the effect of the diggings on village life was recorded in an account of the life story of Annie Macpherson. She moved into Little Eversden in 1858 with her parents to stay with their aunt.

> *"Just at this time the discovery was made that the fossils embedded in the clay soil of that neighbourhood formed, when ground to powder, a valuable manure for the land. Within a week about 500 rough miners and labourers poured into the quiet little villages, and the pressing need was felt of efforts to civilise and evangelise these men, not only for their own sakes, but to save the rustics of the villages from the contamination brought about by the drunken and loose habits of these invaders of their peace, and the immorality induced by the absence of any provision for lodging and sleeping accommodation for this unprecedented addition to the countryside."*

(Birt, L. (1931), *'The Children's Home Finder'*, London, p.9)

Maybe hoards of strangers descended on Arlesey but documentation of their impact on local village life has not been found. However, in other parishes these gangs were not entirely welcomed. Samuel Hopkins, the village grocer, postmaster and deacon to the Bassingbourn Congregational Church reported how

> *"...the discovery of coprolites... brought together a large influx of persons from all parts who were employed in digging them out of the earth. These persons were the refuse of society, and with few exceptions, were extravagant, intemperate, licentious, depraved and atheistical in their conduct. One of the principal employers was an avowed Infidel. By his example, by his distribution of pernicious writings and tracts, the minds of many became infected.*
> *The employment of these men (who are called Diggers)*

was lucrative. They earned much money, they required lodgings. Consequently they were spread all over the village and neighbourhood. Whenever they lodged, with a few exceptions, they caused a spiritual blight, the people became indifferent, careless in their attendances and unconcerned about their state; many who were hopeful characters fell away and gave evidence that an increase in riches is destructive of spiritual life.

To meet this gigantic evil, fresh evangelistic efforts were put forth, with the aid of surrounding friends, a large room was built for the use of these people for reading and instruction on week days and for divine service on the Sunday evenings, an evangelist was also employed to converse with them, or preach, distribute tracts and endeavour to restrain them, but drunkenness and immorality so awfully and universally prevailed that these efforts for their salvation were fruitless. Some of these characters would occasionally attend our services, one or two were brought under the power of the word and were added to the church.

To prevent the spread of infidelity Mr. Harrison gave lecture series with the assistance of other visiting ministers. The increase of population by the opening of the coprolite pits and the widespread wickedness caused thereby made his position more trying than any of his predecessors experienced yet he ceased not to warn the wicked."

(Hopkins, Samuel, Original MS in possession of Deacon of Bassingbourn Congregational Church, pp.210ff., Xerox copies in Cambs. Collection and CUL)

Rev. L. Jenyns of Bottisham Hall near Cambridge knew enough about the local industry to prepare a paper on the subject to read at a meeting of the Bath Field Club. He had been Charles Darwin's tutor at Cambridge University and was clearly very interested in the fossil industry. His notes show how he considered that it brought immense wealth to the area but he concluded:-

"...The consideration of the subject impresses us with a sense of the vast an important results following in some cases from most trifling incidents - Here in this case vast mines of wealth discovered so to speak from a man of science handling and observing in his walks what to others was but an ordinary stone - It teaches us how all observation and learning may lead to most important practical results - but it teaches a far higher lesson too. - As we look at these shapeless stones they seem to have a voice which leads our thoughts above the world to its One great Ruler - even the stones cry out and speak to us how through countless ages He prepared the world for man - His greatest and last creation - how for man He hid beneath the surface of the earth treasure houses of precious things which from time to time he brings forth for their welfare and provision. Yes in these little stones let us see the tracings of the fingers of God - and evidence of His mighty power - and evidence of his care for man - one of the countless proofs of His lowing Providence with which the earth is filled - and so to Him be all the glory."

(CCRO. Lecture notes of Rev .L. Jenyns, Bottisham)

In his speech he assessed the advantages and disadvantages of the diggings on the local people. He argued that they had

"... led to a manifest improvement in their condition in some respects, while it has had an unfavourable influence upon it in others. The introduction of a new kind of labour, which may be carried on all through the winter, brings the men plenty of work, and from the nature of that work, higher wages than they were formerly used to. And this is greatly of the advantage of those men who are steady and provident. Earning from 15s. to 20s. (£0.75 -£1.00) a week, - even young boys of

fourteen years getting 10s. (£0.50) for barrow work, - they not only live better, and a re visibly better clothed on Sundays, but they are able to save. Further, some of the more intelligent labourers have become good mechanics, and have got to having the charge of steam-engines and other machinery; while the genius of the men generally has been much stimulated by endeavouring from time to time to discover the best and most a advantageous methods of digging out the nodules, washing them, and carrying on other operations. The unfavourable result of these diggings is that drinking has increased. The men work very regularly their own time, and have their allotted beer - two or three pints a day - whilst engaged in it, which is not much more than the labour requires. But leaving work every day at four in the afternoon, and on Saturdays always at twelve at noon, they have much time at their disposal, inducing idle habits, and tempting them to sit long at public houses on their way home.

...The diggings have also, to a certain degree, operated unfavourably for ordinary farm work. The labour is considerably affected in some places, though the scarcity of the men, at first much felt, has been partly corrected by immigration, families coming in from the woodland parts of the county to settle where the hands are most wanted. Formerly the price of labour was regulated by the price of wheat, now in the neighbourhood in which my informant lives, he tells me, for the last six or eight years, it has been affected simply by the supply and demand for labour, a principle before unknown in this part of the country. All the able-bodied men go "a-fossilling" as it is called; and they scarcely ever go back to their former employments. The farmers, consequently, are obliged not only to pay a higher rate of wage than formerly, but to put up, in many instances, with the old and very young, the latter being taken away from school at proportionately early age, and thereby receiving detriment to their education. Boys of fourteen years get

to consider themselves men in all their habits, and to assume an air of independence, not favourable either to their manners or morals, before they are much more than half grown up."

(Jenyns, Rev. L. (1866), 'On the Phosphatic Nodules obtained in the Eastern Counties, and used in Agriculture.' *Proc. Bath Nat. Hist. Field Club*, p.17,112)

The Cambridge University and District Coprolite Visiting Societies were established to raise funds to print and distribute religious tracts among the diggers, hold prayer meetings, set up Temperance Societies, open coffee houses, reading rooms and "schools" where moral and religious instruction was given. Cambridge- professors and students came from the University to give talks to the men and win quiet influence over them. Over in the Eversdens Annie Macpherson met with a measure- of success in her evangelical work.

"It was not easy for a timid woman to approach these rough characters... at first her efforts were received - with sneers and scoffing. Often she would spend hours in prayer before she could get enough courage to approach a gang of men or even say a word apart... Gradually she won a hearing and a quiet influence- among them..."

(Birt, L. (1931), op.cit. p.14)

During her time here she went down to London and attended a Church mission which provided her with new resources for

...a new power was soon evidenced in Annie Macpherson's work among the coprolite diggers. Clubs, coffee rooms, evening classes, prayer meetings and mission services were carried on, not only in the evenings but at the dinner times in barns if no other place was available, or in the open fields. Many Cambridge- undergraduates took part. At first the speakers were

always men; it was unthought of that a woman should speak publicly... Miss Ellice Hopkins, whose father was a distinguished mathematical tutor at Cambridge, came over to address the gatherings of coprolite diggers and villagers. Ere Annie Macpherson left Cambridgeshire the fossil strata had been almost worked out in that immediate neighbourhood so that only the labour of the regular population was required but the result of her efforts were far reaching. A temperate-, united band of pious young men had been gathered out, full of simple earnestness each seeking to work for God according to his measure of light time and talents."

(Ibid.)

Over in Shillington the vicar, Rev. John Frere, felt that the provision of a coffee shop for the diggers might alleviate some of the problems. Local tradition says that the shop was in fact a shed - a mobile hospital ward that was intended for the Crimean war but which was never sent there. He contacted Mr. Hammond, the bursar of Trinity College, Cambridge. They were the major landowner in Shillington and their permission was needed to have it erected.

Shillington Vicarage
Hitchin
Jan.28 1863

My dear Mr Bursar,

I am about with the aid of a gentleman who takes an interest in the matter to put up a sort of "Reading & Coffee Room" for the working men of the village, with special reference to the case of the "Coprolite diggers," who are not unknown in Cambridgeshire & who have lately invaded us in great force. After having obtained my building (a second-hand Aldershot hut, procured through a Hampshire brother-in-law of mine, a Capt. Chawman) ... and got leave from the landlord (Wm. Wilshere, Chas. Wilshere's elder brother) I find at the eleventh hour, that the land is copyhold of the College... I should be glad to have an assurance that I shall be free to remove this temporary building, if the occasions of the parish require it, to another site...and not lay hold of what I, & those who act with me, are about to give for the benefit of the place & the diminution of drunkenness.

Ever yours very truly,

John A. Frere.

(Trinity College Muniments Box 6.115)

One might have expected the bursar to have agreed to such a request but it was not installed until late in 1864. The local trade directory mentioned that year that

"Efforts are being made by the vicar to establish a library and reading room for the labouring classes and the men employed in the extensive coprolite works in the parish.."

(Kelly's Post Office Directory, 1864)

An investigation of the parish church records might reveal more of this type of work. One wonders whether the records of the Baptists, Wesleyans, Primitive Methodists and the Salvation Army reveal their role in an evangelising mission in this area. Many chapels were opened during this period.

Lawes' workings, as well as at least another two coprolite works in the parish in 1866, provided quite a boost for the village economy. Coprolite diggers were paid up to double the wages of agricultural labourers which caused localised inflation when farmers had to increase their wages to get the harvest in. The increased spending power was often associated with increased beer sales. Beersellers and public houses sprang up and some contractors took beer to the works where men could drink as much as they liked, the cost being deducted on pay night! Their wives and girlfriends would often be waiting at the pub on Friday night before it opened to ensure they got some. There were plenty of opportunities for locals to supplement their income by taking in lodgers. The work was also alternative employment to labouring on the farms, brick works and later cement works. Owners of the latter businesses must have found the coprolite deposit in their pits and no doubt made arrangements to have them sold.

In Lawes' 'Coprolite Raising Statement of Accounts from 1st July to 31st December 1867' it stated

Higham Gobion	£ s. d
For Labour Fixing Mill	28 10 8
Tradesemen's Bills	5 0 9
Incidental Expenses	1 6 0
Division of Salary, J. Weston	7 10 0
Royalty paid Mr Passingham	50 0 0
	£92 7 5

The Coprolites Washed estimated quantity in heaps to wash as per last years accounting 300 tons

Arlsey	
To Labor	107 4 ½
Tradesemen's Bills	28 3 3½
Capital	120 0 4
Well Sinking	12 0 0
Division of Mr Weston's Salary	7 10 0
.. .. Travelling	15 0 0
Royalty paid to Mr Edwards	100 0 0
	£390 0 8

No Coprolites washed estimated quantity in heaps 160 tons

(Rothamsted Research Archive B8.3)

The work involved many young children helping their parents, a common practice in the early 1800s but one which was soon to stop. In Ampthill it was reported that children missed school to work with their parents in the pits. Along with the massive employment of children in factories, workshops and on farms there was concern being expressed about their welfare. It prompted a visit by a government inspector when an official investigation into the employment of young children was set up in 1866. It was reported that in

ARLESEY

46a. "There are three sets of coprolite works, three brickyards and a cement works which have caused a great increase in population, especially in summer, when many houses are crowded. Coprolite employs a good many men, many of whom are strangers. Coprolite works employ some boy leading horses."

(C.U.L. Parliamentary Papers 1867-8 XVII *'1st Report of the Commissioners on the Employment of Children, Young Persons and others in Agriculture'*. pp.108,343,506,518. Evidence to Mr. Portman and his Summary)

Who was responsible for the third set of workings? The financial benefits to Mr. Edwards must have influenced other landowners in the area to have their fields tested. The diggings in Hinxworth and Ashwell were worked along the junction of the chalk and gault clay which ran northwards on two long spurs on either side of the River Rhee. By 1868 the owner of Dunton Lodge Farm wanted to capitalise on the discovery. The farm was tenanted by Simeon Lee and Jonas Carver, and they would normally have been compensated while the land was out of cultivation. Whether their farm labourers were involved in the work is uncertain but it appeared the owner was prepared to sell it with the mining rights, and receive a considerably better price than just as an agricultural estate. When they started is again unknown but the Dunton Estate was put up for sale in July that year and the sale particulars pointed out that,

"Dunton Lodge Farm contains VALUABLE BEDS OF COPROLITES, which are being worked by the owner.

There are also large Deposits on the Church Farm and some on Millow Bury."

(BCRO. WG.2359)

Subsequent evidence suggests that Lawes won a lease as a few months later Beaver noted, *"On the 5th October 1868 I am coprolite surveying at Dunton Lodge Farm near Biggleswade for J. B. Lawes."* By November he reported that, *"Coprolite work in full swing,"* and by the following year admitted that *"All 1869 J.B. Lawes' people very busy in diggings which take up a great deal of my time."* (Hitchin Museum, G. Beaver's diaries, pp.86a,87a.) No evidence in the way of maps or correspondence has emerged that would locate the extent of the Dunton Lodge diggings but it seemed they must have been exhausted by August 1874 as the farm was again put up for sale. There was no mention of coprolites in the sale particulars.

In March 1870, the master of St. John's College, Cambridge, allowed the tenant of part of the Manor of Renwick (sic), a licence to raise the coprolites on his copyhold land. Whether the farmer raised the seam using his own agricultural labourers or got a coprolite contractor to do the work is not known. Details of the extent of the diggings haven't come to light.

In the same month, Sophia Edwards of Eatonsbury, the Lady of Arlesey Manor, gave a licence to David Dear, to raise the coprolites for three years from one rood, *"all that piece or parcel of land or grounds in Little Field in Arlesey... and to restore the land proper to cultivation."* She must have been Bedford Edwards' relation? One wonders why Mr. Dear only paid her £10, the equivalent of £40 an acre. It was far less than the average rate of £100 per acre. (BCRO. IN 130; BW 854)

In the same year, 1870, Beaver made a visit to the Arlesey coprolite workings on behalf of Mr. Lawes. Unfortunately, his diary entries gave no details as to their location or any of his measurements. (Hitchin Library, Beaver's Diary,p.93a)

Over the first decade of coprolite diggings the upward trend of population growth continued. Whilst a 16.5% increase was virtually identical to the increase in the previous decade it is interesting looking at some individual parishes. Only Henlow and Upper Stondon experienced a decline. Could men and boys have moved from these parishes to find work in the pits? Apart from Campton and Shefford all the rest had increases over double figures. Arlesey saw a 44% increase to 2019. It was the largest fluctuation that century and almost certainly was linked to the diggings.

Changing Population of Bedfordshire Coprolite Vilages

	1861	1871	% change
Astwick	64	64	0.0
Dunton	518	570	10.0
Edworth	99	119	20.2
Eyeworth	149	169	13.4
Langford	1086	1250	15.1
Arlesey	1401	2019	44.1
Campton	529	570	7.8
Shefford	1015	1111	9.5
Clifton	1478	1700	15.0
Henlow	1011	997	-1.4
Meppershall	541	613	13.3
Shefford Hardwick	56	71	26.8
Shitlington	1788	2173	21.5
Upper Stondon	66	47	-28.8
Stotfold	2071	2352	13.6
Total	11872	13825	16.5

According to the 1871 census there were 347 men and boys engaged in the coprolite industry in Bedfordshire. 84% of them were in this area. It is quite likely that many who were described as labourers were involved. Similarly, many described as agricultural labourers could have been engaged by the farmer to work the deposit over the winter months. Almost 50% of those involved were in Shillington where 154 men and boys were recorded. In Arlesey there were fifty-one men and boys described as involved. The notes at the front of the Arlesey census stated that here were *"also cottages in the Brickyards and Coprolite Works."* The diggings were one of the major occupations alongside brickmaking and agricultural labour . The eldest was 55-year old Edmund Clark and the youngest, 13-year old John Albone. The average age was 23.7 and the table below shows their age structure.

Age of Arlesey's Coprolite Labourers 1871

13 - 19	5
20 – 25	18
26 – 35	18
35 - 45	7
Over 45	3

(BCRO. 1871 census)

Confirming the influx of labourers 39-year old Samuel Arnold from Hinxworth lived in a *"Caravan for the Coprolite."* Five men, just under 10%, were boarders which would have provided additional income to some of the residents. It is possible of course that some of those who were from outside the area moved out temporarily when the enumerator moved in. Analysis of their home parishes shows that 60% were local Arlesey people, 20% were from nearby parishes but the rest were attracted here from outside the county. This can be seen in the table below.

Home Locations of Arlesey's 1871 Coprolite Labourers.

Arlesey	30
Shefford	2
Stotfold	2
Clifton	1
Hinxworth	1
Ireland	1

Langford	1
Shillington	1
Cambs.	3
Gloc.	1
Hants.	1
Salop	1
Suffolk	1

(BCRO. 1871 Census)

49-year old Henry Pike described himself as *"coprolite labourer and beerseller."* In nearby Shillington, where 154 men and boys were employed in 1871, many of the pubs were taken over by varying classes of diggers. The managers went in one and the diggers in others. (O'Connor, B. (1993), *'The Shillington Fossil Diggings'*, Bernard O'Connor, Gamlingay) There were twenty-nine in Stotfold, twenty-one "copperlight labourers" in Clifton, thirteen in Lower Stondon, six in Meppershall, two in Campton but none in Eyeworth, Dunton or Astwick. (Ibid.)

The early-1870s were the boom years for the coprolite diggings. Coprolite prices increased 20% in two years which led the coprolite contractors to make more arrangements with landowners to extract the deeper deposits. It has been mentioned that the diggers' wages were sometimes double those of agricultural- labourers who only averaged about twelve shillings (£0.60) a week in this neighbourhood. This difference in pay and potential spending power in the beerhouses probably caused some jealousy - as well as the fact that they worked shorter hours. At this time there was a general increase in newspapers, journals and magazines. An increase in literacy amongst some of the agricultural workers led to a growing awareness of the different wage levels across the country and how little farm labourers received in comparison with industrial workers. There was unrest amongst the labouring classes demanding better pay and conditions. Incendiarism had been common in this area earlier in the century following large lay offs by local farmers as they introduced labour saving machinery.

By early summer 1871 the unrest had spread to Ashwell. The profits being made by those in charge led some coprolite labourers to take action. It was in the pages of the liberal Potton Journal that the following incident was reported.

*"**ASHWELL** - We understand there has been a strike at the coprolite works in this neighbourhood, and that now labourers are in demand at the increased rate of wages. It is an opportunity for many to improve their position."*

(Potton Journal, June 17th 1871)

Why was there no mention of it in the Bedfordshire Journal, Cambridge Chronicle, Cambridge- Independent or Royston Crow? It would not have been considered the done thing in those days for these conservative papers' sponsors to be seen to be encouraging such action.

Just southwest of the village of Campton there were pits opened south of Highlands Lodge Farm. The local historian, D. J. Cadman, in his history of the village made a brief reference to them being raised for use as fertiliser.

"To obtain a correctly balanced supply of soil nutrients, farmers began to use other fertilisers including guano from Peru and superphosphate. A local supply of phosphate was found in coprolites. These were nodules formed around animal remains, possibly including the dung of dinosaurs. They were found at the top of the gault clay and dug from shallow pits in many different parts of the county and groups of these were on Highlands Farm. The nodules were washed in a water-filled hole and transported on a short stretch of narrow-gauge track to the Gravenhurst Road. From where they went by cart to Shefford Station and by rail to a crushing mill - possibly the one at Royston."

(Cadman, D. J. (1975), 'Campton',)

By May 1872 Lawes' workings on Mr. Edwards' land extended towards adjoining property belonging to St. John's College, Cambridge. The map in the illustrations shows there was about four and a half acres to be worked on land east of *"Arlsey (sic) Street."* This was land in the possession of a number of tenants. As other licences had been obtained on the two adjoining manors, Mr. Reyner, the College bursar, received an application from Mr. Dear to dig 0a.2r.20p, part of the 2a.1r.21p. allotment. He got it for £75, the equivalent of £120 per acre. This was 300% more than what he was paying the Lady of the Manor.

The Cambridge colleges owned thousands of acres of land around Cambridge and made many tens of thousands of pounds from coprolites. To them it was a major source of income. Having coprolite land in Arlesey was a welcome source of income for St. John's. The lease was drawn up by Clement Francis, a Cambridge solicitor. Mr. Dear had to compensate the Lord of the Manor a third of the proceeds. (St. John's Coll. Box 162 7/1) Clement Francis, like Messrs. Bidwell and Beaver, had a lucrative practice across the coprolite belt as well as owning a large estate on the fens. Many entrepreneurial Victorians speculated on the industry buying up plots of coprolite land to then be sold at a profit to coprolite contractors or others. Maybe Francis had bought manorial rights here?

If Mr. Bidwell's suggestion was true that the yield was about 250 tons per acre and the manure manufacturers at that time did pay £3 per ton, then it is easy to see that before paying this compensation, labour and capital costs, Mr. Dear would have likely made several hundred pounds, a very profitable enterprise.

In 1872 a group of businessmen bought Lawes' Chemical Manure Company and coprolite contracts for £300,000. This was an enormous fortune in those days.

£100,000 was used to set up Lawes' Agricultural Trust, a fund which established the world's first agricultural research station at Rothamsted. After a year or so managing the coprolite side of the business they considered that the increased labour costs made it not as profitable as they had hoped. Their 1873 account books show that the Astwick workings had cost £183 15s.3d. to open and develop and that there were 7a.3r.28p. left to work. (Lawes Chem. Manure Co. Private Ledger, I, p.98, Valence House Museum, Dagenham)

The fossil seam to the west was also being exploited in the early-1870s. In Stondon the parish glebe land was worked. The vicar, Richard Hicks, pointed out in a note to the Bishop of Ely that he had received £270 for the coprolites, money that had been invested in Queen Anne's Bounty. (CUL.EDR.C3/25) Whether the tenant farmer was working the pits or a coprolite contractor had won a lease is unknown as no further documentation has come to light. It is possible that Lawes won the agreement as his company records show his involvement in Stondon. The 1873 report on the profitability of the coprolite side of the business shed some light on the Stondon works. £2,324. 02 had been expended on developing the works, more than £700 more than those at Shillington! (Valence House Museum, Dagenham, Lawes Chemical Manure Co. Private Ledger, I, 1873, p.98) This would have included the tools like pickaxes, shovels, crow bars, planks, dog irons (supports for the planks across the trenches), carts, barrows, horses, tramways, washmills, steam engines, pumps etc. It revealed that there were a further 11a.2r.15p. yet to be worked.

By 1874, unable to pay Lawes the full amount, the company allowed him to take over the coprolite contracts. He then arranged for the work to continue and profited from the sale of the coprolites to the new company. Digging several acres a year meant that the seam in Stondon was exhausted by the mid-1870s. Whether they were on the parish glebe is uncertain as in 1876 as Beaver reported,

"During this year (1876) I have been very busy with

sundry crop, coprolite and other surveys - viz. Lady Cowper's & Christ's Hospital estates at Stondon for coprolites - Hunsdon Lodge Farm."

(Beaver, op.cit, p.111b.)

No records of the Cowper estate have come to light and enquiries with Christ's Hospital have not turned up anything. Having washed and sorted the fossils, the labourers piled them up in great heaps by the roadside until they were ready for horse-drawn tumbrils to carry them to the station. Ten years after the start of the industry there was a major accident on the railway at Arlesey siding (BCRO. Photograph ref. Z50/2/4).

"In the latter end of December 1876 a railway accident occurred at Arlesey siding, five miles from Hitchin on the Great Northern Railway. A pick up goods train consisting of 25 trucks arrived at the siding from Peterborough. The driver was stopped at a signal box by the siding where some trucks for London were standing., 22 trucks of the goods train had already been backed into the west siding when a truck laden with 9 tons of coprolite, in crossing over the fixed points fouled the metals and the wheels becoming embedded in the permanent way, two succeeding trucks laden with sand and the guards brake also left the metals and this arrested the shunting operations. Lights were lighted and a repair gang got to work, but an express train crashed into it killing the driver (Thomas Pepper), stoker, and three others, while a further 30 were injured."

(BCRO. 'Bedford Town and Townsman')

Accidents in the pits themselves were a common phenomena. Careful analysis of the contemporary newspapers might shed more light on these. The local historian, F. Brittain, pointed out that one of his ancestors, William Brittain, started work in the coprolite industry in 1873 at the age of seven but, when it fell into decline, he went into farming and gardening.

(Brittain, F. (1972) *'It's a Don's Life'*, Heinemann) In his account of Feeny Arnold, one of the local characters from that period, he noted that,

> "When he, Feeny Arnold, was in his twenties he left the farm and worked for a company that was digging for coprolites in the neighbourhood. One day, when he was digging in a fairly deep pit, the earth suddenly fell in on him and crushed his legs and other parts of his body so badly that he was left a cripple for life. This was long before the days of the workmen's Compensation Act, and Feeney, who did not receive a penny from his employers was faced with the prospect of utter destitution."

(Brittain, F. 'F. A.' *Beds. Mag.* Vol. 2.138)

During 1875 Samuel Bedford Edwards, following the death of his father of the same name, arranged the sale of Arlesey Bury Manor. The sale took place at the Sun Hotel in Hitchin at 4.00pm on Tuesday 1st June 1875 under the instruction of Messrs Brittan, Press & Inskip, Solicitors of Small Street in Bristol. The auctioneer was George Nichols. Maybe Lawes was at the auction. Seven plots totalling 96a. 2r.26p. were described in the sale particulars as having *"coprolites under the surface"*. It was mostly market garden ground, arable and plantation on Shawmoor, Brookland's Field, Gaylor's Field, Chism and Gravel Pit Field. New rights of way were to be permitted across the fields to provide access to the road between Arlesey and Stotfold. (Document in possession of Geoff Page, Arlesey)

Interestingly, it was bought by Messrs Lysaght, Inskip and Company. On the 29th December 1876 John Lysaght, a manufacturer from Bristol, George Nichols, an auctioneer and surveyor and James Inskip signed an agreement with a Mr. Frederick Smith, a coprolite merchant from Royston. Mr. Smith paid them £3,215 for the 21a.3r.23p. market garden ground and plantation on Shawmoor, No. 42 on enclosure map, near the Stotfold parish boundary. This was the equivalent of £150 an acre, the highest recorded royalty in Bedfordshire. He would have benefited from a proposed new road running from the corner of the field to the Hitchin Road. (BCRO. SH 111/4)

In Rev. Phillips' history of Stotfold he stated that the diggings were at their height about 1860 - 1880 and "*many thousands of tons of coprolite were dug every year, and at one pit alone as many as 300 persons were employed, either in digging or sorting.*" (Phillips, op.cit. p. 50)

With Smith's, Lawes', Dear's and probably other contractors workings there were numerous job opportunities in the area. A description of Shillington in an 1876 trade directory stated that there were 1,400 people working in the industry. (Harrods Directory 1876) With all the workings in and around Arlesey potentially several thousand would have been employed in the area. Records show that Lawes had contracts with landowners in Arlesey, Astwick, Gravenhurst, Henlow, Meppershall, Shillington, Stondon and Higham Gobion. There were other workings in Ampthill, Millbrook and further west in Barton-le-Clay, Brickhill, Billington, Eggington and Stanbridge. With other contractors and farmers engaged in the work this area was clearly a major operation indeed, the centre of the Bedfordshire coprolite belt.

Kelly's Post Office Director included in its 1878 description of Edworth that coprolite diggings were still going on. Beaver's diary entry revealed other parishes where it was still being carried on.

"*Coprolite diggings are carried on this year at Pirton Grange, Henlow Oldfield, Astwick Bury, Ashwell & Stondon... all of which have required attention and have given a very acceptable supply of work.*"

(Beaver, op.cit.p.117a)

However, the boom did not last. There were problems

ahead. In the latter half of the 1870s there were four consecutive years of bad weather, heavy rain and poor harvests which badly affected farmers and coprolite diggers alike. The wet soil was difficult to work, harvests were ruined and yields dropped The farmers' economic problems were exacerbated by the then Tory government's introduction of Free Trade. Vast quantities of cheap meat and grain surpluses from the American and Canadian Prairies and the Argentinean Pampas were shipped into Great Britain. Home prices plummeted. Farmers tried to arrange rent reductions. Some managed to get 30%. Many went into arrears and bankruptcies were common. Many farms went untenanted for years and there were large-scale redundancies. The Agricultural Depression had set in.

The wet weather made the work in the coprolite pits dangerous as well as incurring additional pumping costs. On top of this newly discovered rock phosphate from Charleston, Carolina started to be shipped into British ports. Much cheaper than coprolites and with a higher phosphate content it caused prices to drop to less than £2.00 a ton. Many coprolite contractors curtailed their operations. Men were laid off and contractors asked to be allowed reductions of their leases. Some landowners refused and forced them into bankruptcy. Pits were abandoned, plant and machinery was locked in sheds or left to rust in the fields. Open pits became swimming pools. Coprolite labourers added to the numbers of unemployed.

Despite cheaper overseas supplies of phosphates the manure manufacturers suffered too. Farmers were not buying fertilisers to grow food they couldn't sell. The prices of "super" fell to below £5.00 a ton. This downward spiral in trade came full circle when the manure manufacturers reduced their purchases of the overseas phosphates. The market for "super" had collapsed.

By late-1881 there was a brief revival. The weather had improved but the main reason was that inland manure manufacturers started making bigger purchases of coprolites, albeit at lower prices. Many of the directors and shareholders were farmers or landowners with coprolite holdings. In the case of the Farmers Manure Company of Royston their managing director still had vast reserves of coprolites on his land in Bassingbourn. Not only did it supply his business with a cheap raw material but also provided work for unemployed labour as well as welcome personal income. (O'Connor, B. (1999), *The Dinosaurs on Bassingbourn Fen',* Bernard O'Connor, Gamlingay) There was also the fact that freight rates had gone up so buying in imported phosphates was not quite as economic as for the coastal manufacturers. Cheaper coprolites were still available.

The 1881 census revealed the scale of the Depression. The upward trend of the previous decades had ceased. Although there had been a small increase of 169 in the local parishes, most experienced reductions in population. Arlesey experienced a drop of 111 whilst Meppershall, Shillington, Upper Stondon and Stotfold saw some increase. Could it have been that unemployed diggers moved over to those parishes to find work?

Changing Population of Bedfordshire Coprolite Villages

Coprolite Parishes	1871	1881	1891	1901
Astwick	64	49	54	62
Dunton	570	477	434	392
Edworth	119	112	100	86
Eyeworth	169	170	140	121
Langford	1250	1242	1183	1187
Arlesey	2019	1908	2108	2221
Campton	570	555	448	437
Shefford	1111	1070	990	874
Clifton	1700	1458	1374	1283
Henlow	997	932	879	905

Meppershall	613	778	650	655
Shefford Hardwick	71	53	65	62
Shitlington	2173	2226	1873	1702
Upper Stondon	47	7272	47	58
Stotfold	2352	2892	3004	2768
Total	13825	13994	13349	12813

(Census returns 1871-1901))

The 1891 census confirmed the demise of the coprolite industry. Of the 47 recorded as involved in Bedfordshire 36 were engaged in Potton. There were only seven in this area, four in Meppershall and three in Shillington. There was no mention of anyone involved in Arlesey or the other local parishes. (BCRO. 1891 census) The diggings came to an end a few years later.

In 1894 the Quarries Act introduced stricter health and safety conditions for pits over twenty-five feet deep. This further increased costs. The remaining coprolite labourers were laid off. Some gained employment in the cement works. Cadman suggested that many in this area were able to get back into farm labour on those farms which concentrated on market gardening. Others left the area to find work in the growing industrial towns.

> "With expanding markets in the North and London, now easily accessible by rail, market gardeners who were almost free from overseas competition did not suffer as much in the depression as did the arable and stock farmers."

(Cadman, D. J. (1975), op.cit.)

There were several references in Victorian geological literature to the coprolites being extracted in the Shefford area but they did not give exact locations of the pits, nor the dates it was worked. The geologist, Jukes-Brown, in his description of Britain's Cretaceous rocks mentioned that the coprolites were worked in 1874. They were

> "...found at or near the base of the gault (clay) in sufficient quantity to pay for working in several parts of the county, e.g. at Shefford in Beds." "...The nodules lay in a bed of light-grey clay, and were scattered through a thickness varying from 9 inches to 2 feet... Belemnites minimus was so abundant that they had to be picked out by hand after the nodules were washed and before they were sent away."

> (Jukes-Brown (1900), 'Cretaceous Rocks of Great Britain', *Mem. Geol. Surv.* p.430,432; See also Strahan, Flitt and Denham, 'Mineral Resources of G. B.' 1915-19, *Mem. Geol. Surv.*, p.20)

Today little remains as evidence of this short-lived but significant industry in Arlesey's 19th century past. Many would have profited from it, both labourers and gentry. The local economy was stimulated during the late-1860s and early 1870s and then fell into decline with the industry's demise in the late 1870s. Although there was a brief revival in the 1880s, the demise of the diggings in the early 1890s led to further economic decline and out migration.

During the period that the diggings were going on in this area very few archaeological finds were reported. As today, most finds probably went straight into the pockets of the diggers. Then, there was a ready market for interesting finds. However, those that were reported, give evidence of Roman occupation in the area.

> "*Near Astwick a number of human skeletons were found during coprolite digging; near them were 10 Samian vessels. A sword, a shield boss, a number of spearheads and a knife were found with the skeletons. The site is on flat ground near a stream. (O.S. 216385)*"

> (*Trans.Herts.Nat.Hist.Soc.* IV (1886); Fox, (1923),

'Archaeology of Cambs.' p.267)

Where the finds went is unknown but in many cases where the diggings unearthed treasures like this, the diggers sold them on Cambridge Market. In Stondon, further evidence of Roman occupation was provided by the diggers. A long, thin bronze object, thought to be an ear pick from Roman times, was donated to the Cambridge Museum of Archaeology and Anthropology. It was reported to have come *"from Lord Cowper's coprolite diggings"*. Certainly there were workings on Lady Cowper's estate on Hunsdon Lodge Farm in 1876 but documentation of Lord Cowper's agreements has not emerged. (Cambridge Museum of Arch. and Anth. IDNO D)

During the forty years or so of the coprolite industry entrepreneurs like Lawes and Smith dominated the work in this area and probably worked over a thousand acres between them. Paying landowners an average £100 an acre it would have amounted to approximately £100,000. Selling the coprolites at an average of £2.50 a ton before labour and capital costs they could have made hundreds of thousands of pounds.

They and other farmers and contractors' business stimulated other trades. Local carpenters gained useful work in the erection and repair coprolite sheds, making coprolite trucks and cutting timer for planks and supports. Blacksmiths would have had work making and repairing tools and shoeing horses. Surveyors, solicitors and auctioneers made good business out of the arrangements between landowners and contractors. Bankers would have profited from the loans made to speculators in the industry. Brewers, shopkeepers and other traders would have benefited from the increased spending power generated by the industry. Carters would have made a good trade taking coprolites to the mills and stations. Colchester established an iron works in Bassingbourn where much of the coprolite plant and machinery was made. Cottages were constructed, churches were built or renovated and much improvement was done during this period. What was done with the money realised by the diggers is not known. Purchasing land, building houses and renovating property was common but probably a lot would have been spent on food, clothes and drink. The diggings brought this area a level of prosperity never experienced before or since. Maybe this account will bring to light other aspects of the industry in Arlesey and surrounding parishes but it has helped to keep alive the memory of the hundreds of local people involved in this unusual business.

Bibliography

Anonymous, 'The Study of Abstract Science Essential to the Progress of Industry,' *Memoirs of Geological Survey,* Mineral Statistics, Vol. I, 1850?, pp.40-1

Anonymous, 'The Farming of Cambridgeshire,' *Royal Agric.Soc.*1847, p.71

Beaver, G. diaries in Hitchin Museum, p.73a

Bedfordshire Times, May 18th 1962. from an original article in 1878

Birt, L. (1931), *'The Children's Home Finder',* London, pp.9,14

Brittain, F. 'F. A.' *Beds. Mag.* Vol. 2.138

Cadman, D. J. (1976), *'Campton - Story of a Bedfordshire Village',* David Cadman

Cambridge Independent Press, 18th January, p.3

Clutterbuck, Robert, (1877), 'The Coprolite Beds at Hinxworth,' *Trans. Watford Natural History Soc.* Vol. 1. p.238;

Druce, D. (1881), *'Report on Cambridgeshire,'* Royal Commission of Agriculture. p.365;

Dyke, G.V. (1993), *'John Lawes of Rothamsted'* Hoos Press, Harpenden, p.15

Ellison, D. 'Coprolites in the Orwell area,' part of *Orwell History Topics*; Ref. Latter Day Saints Millennial Star, passim, Fertiliser Manufacturers Association, (FMA.) Peterborough, Railway Rates 1888-94; Commercial matters 1890-98

Fowle, K. (1992), *'Coton through the Ages',* private publication

Fox, (1923),*'Archaeology of the Cambridge Region',* CUP. p.267

Gathercole, A. F. (1959), 'Fenland Village,' *Fisons Journal,* No.64 Sept. pp.24-9

Graham, J. (1839), *'A Treatise on the Use and Value of Manure',* London p.6

Grove, R. (1976), *"The Cambridgeshire Coprolite Mining Rush'* Oleander Press, Cambridge

Hailstone, Rev. J. (1816), 'Outlines of the Geology of Cambridgeshire', *Phil. Trans. Royal. Soc.,* pp.243-250

Hanscomb, C. E. (1967), *'Common Blood,'* Queen Anne Press, pp.158-9

Hopkins, S. Original MS in possession of Deacon of

Bassingbourn Congregational Church, pp.210ff., Cambs.
Collection and CUL

Jenyns, Rev. L 'On the Phosphatic Nodules obtained in the
Eastern Counties, and used in Agriculture.' *Proc. Bath Nat. Hist.
Field Club,* 1866 p.17,112 and Lecture notes in CCRO.

Jukes-Brown (1900), 'Cretaceous Rocks of Great Britain,' *Mem.
Geol. Surv.* London, pp.430,432

Keatley, W.S. (1976), '*100 years of Fertiliser Manufacture,*'
Fertiliser Manufacturers Association

Kelly's Post Office Directories, 1864, 1876, 1892

Kiln, A. (1969), '*The Coprolite Industry*', Thesis for Putteridge
Bury College, pp. 32, 38, 40-41, 43-4

Kingston, A. (1889) '*Old and New Industries on the Cam,*' Warren
Press, Royston p.16

Kowallis, Gay P. (1970?), '*To the Great Salt Lake from Litlington,*'
Bassingbourn

Lucas, C. (1930), '*The Fenman's World - Memories of a Fenland
Physician,*' (Norwich), pp.25, 31

O'Connor, B. (1990), '*Rothamsted, Lawes and Dinosaurs,*'
Bernard O'Connor, Gamlingay

O'Connor, B. (1993), '*The Shillington Fossil Diggings,*' Bernard
O'Connor, Gamlingay

O'Connor, B. (1998), '*The Dinosaurs on Coldham's Common,*'
Bernard O'Connor, Gamlingay

O'Connor, B. (1998), '*The Dinosaurs on Sandy Heath*', Bernard
O'Connor, Gamlingay

O'Connor, B. (1999), '*The Dinosaurs on Bassingbourn Fen,*'
Bernard O'Connor, Gamlingay

O'Connor, B. (2000), '*The Ashwell Fossil Diggings,*' Bernard
O'Connor, Gamlingay

O'Connor, B. (2001), '*The Suffolk Fossil Diggings,*' Bernard
O'Connor, Gamlingay

Parliamentary Papers 1867-8 XVII '*1st Report of the
Commissioners on the Employment of Children, Young Persons
and others in Agriculture,*' pp.108,343,506,518. Evidence to Mr.
Portman and his Summary

Pierre, W.H. and Norman, A.G. (Eds.) (1953), '*Soil Fertiliser
Phosphorous in Crop Nutrition,*' New York Academic Press, p. ix

Phillips, Rev. G. C. H. (1951), '*Stotfold, Beds.*' Bancroft Press, Hitchin, p. 50

Porter, E. notebooks in Cambridge Folk Museum 15/64-65

Potton Journal, June 17th 1871

Reid, C. (1890), 'Phosphate Nodule Bed,' *Mem. Geol. Surv.* p.16

Royston Crow, 26th September, 1884; 18th May 1888

Strahan, Flitt and Denham, 'Mineral Resources of G. B.' 1915-19, *Mem. Geol. Surv.*, p.20

Tye, W. (1930),'Birth of Fertilizer Industry', *Fisons Journal*,pp.3-10

Voelcker, A. (1862), '*The International Exhibition at Paris,*' p.149

Whitaker, W. and Skertchley (1891) 'The Geology of parts of Cambridge and of Suffolk,' *Mem.Geol.Surv.*

Whitaker, W. (1921), 'Water Supply of Cambs.' *Mem. Geol. Surv.* p.84

www.ingramcontent.com/pod-product-compliance
Lightning Source LLC
Chambersburg PA
CBHW060125050426
42448CB00010B/2022